ISBN # 978-0-9809248-0-0

Published by: Spindel & Associates Inc. Toronto, Ontario, Canada. www.spindelconsulting.com

Copies may be obtained on Amazon.com or from the publisher.

Cover and internal design by Sandy Kay.

Disclaimer

The information contained in this book is based on a compilation of structured and informal interviews, a review of literature on this subject, and the author's observations. Names and some information included in the case examples that may serve to identify individuals have been changed to ensure confidentiality. The author and publisher accept no responsibility or liability for information contained in this book that may coincidentally resemble any actual situations, individuals, or events.

It is always advisable to seek legal advice when addressing issues of psychological harassment in the workplace, therefore readers are urged to use information contained in this book in a cautious and responsible manner. Neither the author nor the publisher assumes responsibility or liability for any type of damage caused or alleged to be caused to any person, organization, group or entity by information contained in this book. Any misunderstanding, use, or misuse made of the material in this book is the sole responsibility of the reader.

LE/
31!
TC

D1546904

Acknowledgements

Special thanks go to the individuals who so kindly agreed to be interviewed for this book. For some it represented a re-opening of very painful wounds, something that they were willing to undertake in the hope that their stories could help others in similar situations. Their caring, compassion, and courage deserve special acknowledgement. This book would not have been possible without their help.

Thanks also go to my friends, some of my colleagues, and my husband, Harry, who have supported me in the creation of this book. Their insight, understanding, critiques, and helpful suggestions were of great value.

Finally, special thanks to Sandy Kay who designed this book. Her creative talent and humor have been especially appreciated.

Dedication

This book is dedicated to the thousands of people who suffer every day in simply trying to make a living. It is for them, and for the managers who want to change workplace battlefields into places of civility and support that this book was written.

TABLE OF CONTENTS

Preface

Albert Einstein had three rules concerning work. He said "out of clutter find simplicity, from discord find harmony, and in the middle of difficulty lies opportunity". His wisdom echoes throughout this book in the stories of those who have had to fight their way through workplace battlegrounds to simply bring home a paycheck.

For many, having to survive the mental torture inflicted by bullies and harassers in modern day workplaces, has led to positive life changes that they would likely not have made had they not had to endure what they did. The old adage that what does not kill us makes us stronger is very true for the survivors of workplace warfare. For those who are still suffering, there is light at the end of the tunnel.

However, the good that can come from horrible suffering does not justify what is occurring in many of today's workplaces. What happens to families where the breadwinner suffers debilitating depression from being the target of a workplace bully? How many people are so badly injured by their co-workers or bosses that they are never able to work again? How many workplaces and insurance companies have to pay out huge settlements to those injured in workplace combat? It is not possible to estimate the damage that bullies and harassers inflict on our workplaces, communities, families, and society.

This book was written to shine a spotlight on what no one wants to talk about or admit – that simply going to work can be a danger to your psychological and physical health, and that not enough managers are effectively confronting this important issue. It is my hope that the information contained herein can help policy makers and managers to make positive changes in organizations and employees' lives.

CHAPTER ONE

What is Psychological Warfare At Work?

You find yourself checking around corners before you proceed, concerned that "the bully" might be nearby. You prepare constantly to defend yourself. You practice how you will counter an attack. You try to use camouflage hoping that if "the bully" can't see you, they won't attack you. You look to the generals for leadership, but there is none. You find yourself alone in the middle of combat, fighting a war you don't understand, of which you wanted no part. Your allies appear to have headed for the hills. And it seems like your weapons aren't working. Your biggest fear is being taken prisoner, and never finding a way out.

It may seem hard to believe, but this is how some employees experience their workplaces - toxic, psychologically violent battlefields where just showing up for work could end in psychological injury. Some feel physically as well as psychologically threatened, unsure of just how far their workplace bully will go in tormenting them.

The bully may be a boss, a co-worker, a customer, client or student. One thing they almost all have in common is that their intent is to psychologically injure or destroy another person. They are willing to engage in a relentless campaign to defeat their target, and they will use all means at their disposal to achieve their objectives.

Targets of this kind of psychological warfare are left weak, emotionally damaged, and physically exhausted. Their ordeal negatively affects family life, and has the capacity to be life threatening. Like survivors of a military campaign, targeted employees come home with symptoms of post-traumatic stress. They can't sleep, they keep reliving their torment, they have distressing physical symptoms. They are, in every respect, veterans of a war, and they have the psychological scars to prove it.

Unfortunately, unlike real combat veterans, there are no special services for them to help piece them back together again after they have been mortally wounded. Others do not see their wounds. They are all on the inside. The torment they feel is hard to explain to others who have not experienced it. The only people who seem to truly understand are other veterans of psychological warfare in the workplace.

Its targets are largely defenseless because the generals in this war are often asleep at the switch. Senior managers of organizations, especially large ones where psychological warfare is more likely to occur, are often oblivious to the toll taken on their front-line workers and middle managers until the battle begins to rage outside their own doors, and by then the battle is largely lost. Many do not want to believe that something this insidious could be occurring in their workplaces, and they dismiss it as "personality conflicts" or disagreements. But the reality is quite different for thousands of workers. Some have been so injured by the psychological mistreatment they have received that, unable to work, they are forced to go on stress leave. Some are never able to return to work. This is no small problem in today's workplaces, and it should not be taken lightly. Ignoring this problem costs companies and organizations millions of dollars a year in lost productivity, sick leave, long term disability and law suits. Perhaps even more injurious is the damage done to an organization's or company's reputation when excellent employees are forced to leave because of the noxious behavior of their bosses or co-workers.

What Constitutes Psychological Warfare?

This kind of psychological warfare is referred to by a lot of different names - non-status psychological or personal harassment, workplace bullying, or mobbing, and it poses a significant danger to workers, supervisors, and to the functional integrity of organizations of all types.

Non-status psychological harassment refers to "vexatious behavior that manifests itself in the form of conduct, verbal comments, actions or gestures that are repetitive, hostile, and unwanted, [that] affect a person's dignity or psychological integrity, and result in a harmful work environment" according to the Commission des Normes du Travail (2005). Quebec is the first jurisdiction in North America to establish a Commission in charge "of the application of the Act respecting labour standards". The Quebec Act establishes the "minimum conditions of employment in the absence of conditions provided for under collective agreement, a contract of employment or a decree." It is a law specifically forbidding psychological harassment in the workplace.

The term "non-status" refers to harassment that is "under the radar" because it is not covered by human rights legislation, and so there are no formally sanctioned remedies for victims in many North American or European jurisdictions. This is one reason that this type of harassment is so widespread - because there is less protection for victims than for sexual harassment or harassment because of discrimination related to race, culture, sexual orientation or other grounds covered by human rights codes (Johnston, 2000).

Psychological harassment is a term that may be used interchangeably with other common terms like workplace bullying or personal harassment, but all represent varying forms of psychological warfare. Workplace bullying is defined by the Workplace Bullying and Trauma Institute (2006), as "repeated, health-impairing mistreatment of one or more persons". It is often driven by a perpetrator's desire to obtain some advantage, or a need to control the targeted individual or group, and it may escalate as others participate, either voluntarily or as coerced. When others become involved, taking the side of the bully and harassing the "target", it is called "mobbing".

Whatever its cause, "workplace bullying undermines legitimate business interests. When bullies' personal agendas dominate; bullying prevents work from getting done" (Ibid). And that is often the objective – to disrupt the normal functioning of an organization, thereby exerting power over others in the workplace.

The Canadian Centre for Occupational Health and Safety (CCOHS, 2006), describes **workplace bullying** in behavioral terms. The parallels to psychological warfare are compelling. Because workplace bullies often engage in a campaign of harassment, they may use various "battle tactics" to defeat their "targets". These include tactics of surprise, stealth, maneuver, and threat or outright aggression.

Tactics of Surprise

Some workplace aggressors sit in wait and attack a target "out of nowhere" at a staff meeting, undermining their credibility, launching personal attacks, or declaring all out psychological war. The target is left shocked, humiliated in front of her or his peers, and at least momentarily unable to respond. Some bullies are so skilled a this kind of surprise attack that any attempt by a target to counterattack or even defend her or himself would be seen as "being defensive", leading others to wonder if the basis for the attacks is true.

Some workplace bullies and harassers remove areas of responsibility from employees, and publicly criticize their work in front of their peers. This creates significant self doubt, especially in a formerly productive employee, and it undermines the target's belief in her or his ability to do the job or fulfill the mission.

Sometimes the opposite tactic is used. By overwhelming someone with an unreasonable workload, or underwhelming them with underwork and underemployment, bullies engage in mind games intended to cause their targets to doubt themselves

This self doubt is further exacerbated by constantly changing work guidelines, or moving the battle lines. By setting impossible deadlines that cause employees to fail, workplace harassers essentially mount a surprise barrage to exhaust their targets. By purposefully withholding or providing incorrect information that makes it impossible for employees to succeed, workplace bullies mount disinformation campaigns.

Tactics of Stealth

Some engage in malicious rumors or innuendo that is not true, or is blown out of proportion. This is generally done without the target's knowledge, behind her or his back. Otherwise known as "backstabbing" this amounts to a well orchestrated propaganda campaign where the target is undermined, their reputation destroyed, and their confidence and will broken.

Some bullies prefer to work through others who act as collaborators, causing pain and discomfort to targets by poisoning other people against them. This is intended to cause conflict between a target and others on their team, or between them and their superiors (Barash 2006; Davenport, Schwartz, & Elliott, 2002). The objective is to undermine and isolate the target, or have them removed from their jobs. Often this occurs by twisting another's words or taking them out of context, spreading untrue or malicious gossip, or putting together bits of information to create a negative picture of the target in the eyes of others.

Some bullies isolate and exclude their targets, preventing them from having access to the information necessary to do their jobs. This is equivalent to cutting supply lines in battle, so that the target eventually loses the ability to fight back. By undermining or deliberately impeding a person from doing her or his work in order to make them look bad, the bully uses sophisticated tactics of sabotage.

Other common stealth tactics include making offensive jokes in person or via e-mail, thereby constantly keeping employees off guard. They may pester, stalk or spy on their targets, thereby engaging in reconnaissance intended to put their targets under the microscope of constant scrutiny, causing them to become nervous and doubt their abilities, or re-consider their every move.

By tampering with personal belongings or work equipment bullies engage in sabotage, further adding to a target's psychological and physical discomfort.

Tactics of Threat and Outright Aggression

In some cases, direct threats are made, or actual physical abuse occurs in an attempt to terrorize the target and, at the same time, any innocent bystanders who may have considered intervening. Most will abandon that notion, terrified that they could be the next target of the bully's campaign.

One particularly effective battle tactic is when the target's confidence is undermined by the use of overwhelming force. The intent is to cause the target to doubt his ability to defend himself. Yelling and using profanity create a tense atmosphere where a target may feel as if s/he is being subjected to overwhelming force.

Perhaps one of the most effective brainwashing techniques used by workplace harassers is to subject their targets to constant criticism without legitimate cause, belittling employees' opinions, especially in front of their peers. In this way, targets can be bullied into silence.

Constant and unwarranted punishment amounts to the use of torture.

Unfairly blocking requests for training, leave, or promotion holds a target in a state of captivity, a form of suspended animation, thereby preventing her or his escape. This "state of captivity' mindset was made famous in a 1971 experiment conducted by Philip Zimbardo of Stanford University and a team of researchers, wherein students were asked to role play guards and prisoners in a mock prison setting. As the students adapted all too readily to their roles, the experiment had to be ended early. Some "guards" appeared to be exhibiting sadistic characteristics, and some of those playing "prisoner" roles were seriously emotionally traumatized during the experiment. Since then, many ethical questions have been raised about conducting even simulated experiments like these, which subject some individuals to captivity, and others to complete dominance. Later researchers, like Peters and Waterman (1981) commented on the disturbing questions about human nature raised by Zimbardo's experiment, as well as a later one conducted by Yale University psychologist, Stanley Milgram, that examined individuals' willingness to obey authority figures, even when following orders seriously contravened their personal ethics (Milgram, 1974). Zimbardo has since written extensively on the subject of how good people appear to turn evil under particular circumstances (Zimbardo, 2007)

By now you are getting the idea. The warfare metaphor may create discomfort in some readers, but it has a deadly accuracy in describing what is happening in many of today's workplaces.

A classic instance of actual psychological warfare in the workplace provides some insight into the dynamics and impact of this phenomenon:

> Sue had worked in a very specialized legal area of government for twenty years. She is a highly talented individual, graduating first in her law school class, and winning the gold medal. Her work had always been highly valued by her employers, and she had established a sterling reputation among senior administrators. It was her sterling reputation and strong ethics – qualities that would normally be viewed as exceptional

by employers, that eventually led to her becoming a target of psychological harassment.

One of her co-workers, an informal or "social" leader of an office clique of which she had never been a part, approached her one day to convince her to take part in a mutiny against her boss. It was clear that the co-worker wanted to be the boss and suggested that the boss was incompetent and had to go. Sue refused to take part, and encouraged the co-worker to work things out with the boss.

Even though Sue had, until then, felt that she was not part of the clique, and that she and a few of her co-workers had had to work in an unwelcoming environment, things deteriorated rapidly after her refusal to take part in the mutiny.

Of course, unbeknownst to Sue, she had inadvertently frustrated the goal of a bully – one who was willing to then orchestrate what amounted to a campaign against her.

Once the bully's tactics succeeded and she became Sue's boss, Sue was given work well below her abilities, being asked to draft laws that a junior could have easily handled rather than someone with her extensive experience. When she requested work assignments in line with her level of expertise she was denied them.

Her relationships with longstanding clients were disrupted, leaving her feeling alone and isolated. She was not given the opportunity to teach courses in her area of expertise that she had always taught, and was not kept in the loop on policy issues – information she needed to do her job.

These bullying tactics are part of very specific "campaign strategies" that have been well documented in other case studies, but also in the literature on psychological harassment. As social animals, human beings need others. Denying them the company of peers or longtime associates can be very damaging to someone's psyche, and is equivalent to being placed on a professional "desert island".

Sue received no recognition and constant criticism for the work she did do. If she requested professional development opportunities, these were denied. In one instance every member of the work team that she led received written thanks from the co-worker, who had, by then, been promoted to become her immediate supervisor, whereas she received written criticism that was shared with her team in an effort to undermine and humiliate her.

Public humiliation and debasement in front of peers is a powerful tool in the hands of a bully. Equivalent to "shaming and shunning", it leaves a target almost afraid to show their face in the workplace for fear of what others are thinking about them. Very few people could withstand this kind of treatment for any length of time.

Sue's supervisor spread vicious gossip about her, suggesting that she was not intelligent, and did not do good work. Sometimes this was shared with her clients, and it caused a change in their behavior towards her. She endured social and professional isolation, belittling, and sabotage.

The cruelty inherent in this kind of approach lies in the ability of the bully to so influence the target's peers and clients, that the culture and climate of the target's world changes in a destructive way – a way that causes the person to begin to doubt her or his own abilities, lose confidence, and question his or her competence. This occurs irrespective of whether or not the person has had a longstanding track record of exemplary work.

Few people have such an unshakeable belief in their own abilities that they could withstand this kind of continuous onslaught.

The harassment to which Sue was subjected seemed to become worse at a time in her life when she was already vulnerable because of deaths in her family.

This "vulnerability" factor appeared in numerous interviews with "targets", as well as in the literature. It is as if some people, sensing weakness or vulnerability, have the capacity to move in like predators for the kill. This "kicking someone when they are down" strategy appears to be quite widespread, and aligns with common battle tactics used in military combat.

Sue, believing that her work would speak for itself, did not, at first, attempt to take action. She was highly committed to her career, experienced it as a calling, and saw what she was doing as her "life's work" while taking great pains to do a superior job. Because of the specialized nature of her legal work, there were very few other career options for her, and she felt trapped. When she did become more assertive in requesting higher level work assignments, she got nowhere. Her efforts were met with silence. There was no forum for her to be able to confront her boss, no clear policies to assist her, and, as she put it, "the bureaucracy punishes a complainer". So she suffered in silence – for years.

This engulfing sense of powerlessness is one shared by many who are targeted for this kind of attack. Targets describe feeling trapped, fearing consequences that could spiral out of control if they attempt to take action to protect themselves or respond. Some argue that "the company" or "the agency" has money to hire good lawyers. They feel outgunned on every level, and realize that if they were to fight, it could well be a losing battle.

The result for Sue, personally, was three bouts of severe depression and a sleep disorder. She was forced to seek therapeutic help because of the repercussions on her mental health that were the direct result of her work environment. Over time she developed another painful medical condition as well that was likely exacerbated by extreme stress.

This state of "captivity", where a person feels that no matter what they do, the consequences will be harsh, is exactly what places many employees who are targeted in an impossible position. If they fight, they are likely to lose since their bullies often have the resources of the company on their side. If they do not fight, they may well suffer severe repercussions in the form of deteriorating mental and physical health, because of which they may lose their jobs. Those being targeted are literally between a rock and a hard place, feeling pinned down, unable to escape to anywhere where self defense might be possible.

With the exception of a couple of co-workers who were also not in the clique and were also treated badly, no one came to Sue's aid.

Later in this book, the "bystander effect" will be discussed in more detail. Bystanders often fail to help someone in Sue's situation, fearing repercussions themselves, or perhaps believing that if no one else is intervening, perhaps they should also "mind their own business".

> *Sue's tormenter, who had been promoted to be her direct supervisor, was described as extraverted, charming, smart, hard working, with a high degree of personal magnetism, but also unable to tolerate views different from her own, and insensitive and mean to those who did not agree with her or do her bidding.*

So often this is the case. Many bullies are highly adaptable and very believable, in that they are able to convince those in senior positions of their competence, and of the "rightness" of their actions, while treating those who report to them abominably. Because of the shame felt by many "targets", senior managers seldom hear of what may really be happening to middle management or front-line employees who report to the "charming" supervisor or manager.

> *Now, unable to deal with the harassment much longer, Sue has sought other employment, and this government department, that badly needs her level of expertise, is likely to lose one of its brightest stars.*

So often it is the "rate busters", the highly capable individuals, envied by others, who fall prey to psychological harassment. They are seen as threats by those who would characterize them as enemies to their own advancement in an organization, and begin to attack them because they are seen to be in the way.

Where someone in authority or a co-worker feels inadequate or challenged by a more competent worker, or sets up a competition with a co-worker, a psychological war has often been declared, whether or not the target knows it. Before long, the target will feel violated and invaded, their defenses tested, and their anxiety increasing.

What Specifically Constitutes Bullying Behavior?

Quine (1999:230) has developed categories of common types of bullying behavior (see table below):

Categories of bullying behavior

Category	Behavior
Threat to professional status	Persistent attempts to belittle or undermine target's work. Persistent unjustified criticism and monitoring of target's work. Persistent attempts to humiliate the target in front of colleagues. Intimidating use of discipline or competence procedures.
Threat to personal standing	Undermining target's personal integrity. Destructive innuendo and sarcasm. Verbal and non-verbal threats. Making inappropriate jokes. Persistent teasing. Physical violence. Violence to property.
Isolation	Withholding necessary information Freezing out, ignoring or excluding Unreasonable refusal of applications for leave, training or promotion
Overwork	Undue pressure to produce work Setting of impossible deadlines

Destabilization	Shifting of goal posts without telling the target
	Constant undervaluing of the target's efforts
	Persistent attempts to demoralize the target
	Removal of areas of responsibility without consultation

Meyers (2006) has summarized what constitutes bullying behavior for the American Psychological Association Monitor: "In a 1998 study in the *Journal of Emotional Abuse* (Vol. 1, No. 1, pages 85-115), Loraleigh Keashly, PhD, a Canadian psychologist who now teaches at Wayne State University, identified seven key components of workplace warfare, or as she defined it, emotional abuse at work. They include behaviors that are:

- Verbal and nonverbal (excluding physical contact).

- Repetitive or patterned.

- Unwelcome and unsolicited by the target.

- Violations of a standard of appropriate conduct toward others.

- Harmful or cause psychological or physical injury to the target.

- Intended to harm or controllable by the actor.

- Exploiting of the actor's position of power over the target."

Cyber-bullying: 21st Century Psychological Harassment

A new form of bullying has emerged with the advent of the Internet. Now employees can bully bosses or other employees, students can bully teachers and principals, and customers can bully service personnel via chat rooms and websites like Facebook. Belsey (2008) has defined cyber-bullying as: "the use of information and communication technologies such as e-mail, cell phone and pager text messages, instant messaging, defamatory personal Web sites, and defamatory online personal polling Web sites, to support deliberate, repeated, and hostile behavior by an individual or group, that is intended to harm others."

While it is the education sector that has received most of the public attention with respect to cyber-bullying, there is nothing to stop employees of any organization from targeting other employees or bosses in this way.

It has become easier to send anonymous threatening e-mails, or establish "anonymous" websites that make fun of someone. Some argue that this is no different from the "poison press" or "gossip around the water cooler" of the past. But when millions of people are able to access information that is nothing more than vicious gossip, that can destroy someone's reputation, prevent them from obtaining work in the future, or cause the destruction of their family life, the results are likely to be far more serious.

On February 12, 2007 *The Toronto Star* featured a front page story of a school principal being "cyber-bullied" by at least eleven students. Both male and female students allegedly posted remarks that were "sexually explicit, derogatory, and demeaning" about the principal, remarks that were so serious that they resulted in lengthy suspensions from school. The principal expressed "disappointment" in the students to whom he referred as "among the school's leaders". These were students who were on the student council, or who were top school athletes. The cyber-bullying allegedly resulted because of the principal's decision to ban personal electronic devices at school.

In another Facebook incident a professor at Fanshawe College in London, Ontario, Canada was also targeted by students in a way that was so severe that she ended up on leave. In investigating workplace practices related to harassment at the community college, the Ontario Ministry of Labour's Occupational Health and Safety Branch laid seven safety act charges against the college (Richmond, December 18, 2006).

Canadian Broadcasting Company (CBC) News reported a particularly harmful type of bullying where someone set up a website targeting a student. David Knight, the young target said: "Rather than just some people, say 30 in a cafeteria, hearing them all yell insults at you, it's up there for 6 billion people to see. Anyone with a computer can see it". The CBC reported this website as asking "others to join in, posting lewd, sexual comments and smearing David's reputation" in a form of cyber mobbing.

The target's mother, a secondary victim of this form of cyber mobbing said: "It's like being stabbed in the back by somebody (and) you have no way of ever finding out who they are, or defending yourself against the words they say. So it's more damaging than a face-to-face confrontation with somebody who is clearly willing to tell you what he or she thinks of you" (CBC News, October 10, 2002).

The impact on David was severe. He isolated himself, not knowing who he could trust. When he and his family attempted to have the website taken down, they ran into one roadblock after another. It seemed that there was no recourse for them.

Belsey (2008) describes cyber-bullying as a more cowardly form of bullying in that perpetrators can more easily "hide behind the anonymity that the Internet provides". It often occurs "outside the reach of" authorities like school boards because it is done on home computers.

Management and Workplace Disagreements Vs Harassment

While it is important to define psychological harassment, it is equally important to outline what it is not.

Psychological harassment is different from the normal exercise of management activities, which may be experienced by some as "boot camp", but which do not rise to the definition of actual warfare. It is the intent, and the repetitive, systematic or strategic quality of someone's mistreatment of, and attacks on another that separates psychological warfare from other common types of workplace disagreements, skirmishes or forms of progressive discipline.

Managers will say that they sometimes need to take corrective action with employees, and may need to implement graduated sanctions for non-performance, and that this could be seen by some as cause to file psychological harassment charges. But this has not been the outcome in Quebec, Canada, where an anti-harassment law, the first of its kind in North America, has been in place since 2004. Of 4700 complaints filed in the first two years the law was in effect, approximately 2400 were found to be substantiated (Commission des Norms du Travail, 2005, Quebec).

It should, therefore, be noted that the normal exercise of management activities, including the "day to day management of discipline, performance at work or absenteeism, the assignment of tasks, the application of the gradation of sanctions and even dismissal [for cause] constitute the legitimate exercise of management right…… These actions do not constitute psychological harassment, provided that the employer does not exercise these rights in an abusive or discriminatory manner" (Ibid).

Sue's employer did exercise these rights in an abusive and discriminatory manner. She was given work assignments well below her level of ability, was unfairly criticized and centered out for censure in front of her peers or team members. She was belittled and isolated. Rumors that were untrue were circulated about her by the person to whom she reported directly. She was punished for failing to take part in a power struggle, for being somewhat shy, but very good at her job. She was resented for her good work that brought prestige and acclaim to her department. Rather than seeing her accomplishments as furthering the work of her department, they were seen as threats to those in positions of authority, justification for attack and the declaration of a psychological war. None of these constitute reasonable management actions, and no manager whose first concern is the well being of the organization and its employees would have allowed these kinds of attacks to go on.

Psychological harassment should also be separated from other common workplace phenomena – periodic disagreements that become heated, or an occasional outburst. These are mere skirmishes that could lead to larger hostilities, but in and of themselves do not add up to psychological harassment unless there is a significant imbalance or abuse of power, and the "effect [is] sufficiently severe" (Tehrani, 2001:81) that one incident might cause considerable harm and be considered to be a declaration of psychological war.

Bullying and Bystanders

One phenomenon that appears repeatedly in the literature is the behavior of bystanders – those who know that someone is being mistreated in the workplace and who do or say nothing, or worse, side with the bully, thereby acting as collaborators.

Bly (1996) says: "the bystander effect is watching some evil take place, but since we are watching with others who are watching, and no one seems to be doing anything about the evil, we go on watching and do nothing about it."

John Darley and Bibb Latane, distinguished U.S. social psychologists, first documented this phenomenon in 1968. Their theory of "diffusion of responsibility" may help to account for why co-workers, aware of someone's mistreatment and distress, fail to speak up. They may simply assume that someone else will, and fail to report it.

Namie and Namie (2003:83-85) point to several other reasons for non-intervention or "bystander apathy". They say that co-workers may privately find the bully's behavior deplorable, but they do not communicate their feelings to their co-workers, and may deny their feelings publicly, not knowing that others also privately share their concerns. This "public/private" view of reality may reinforce a code of silence in a workplace. This silencing climate is extremely harmful to the person being targeted. They may be confused and wonder if their co-workers support the bully.

The authors also suggest that "groupthink" contributes to the problem. If a manager is bullying an employee, or an employee a manager, it is unlikely that other managers will come to the aid of the bullied employee or vice versa because they feel affiliated to the "manager" or "employee" groups.

In some cases, co-workers are simply afraid to confront the bully fearing that they will be centered out next for mistreatment. Fea causes them to remain silent and leave the targeted individual isolated.

The comparisons to civilian populations during a time of warfare are compelling. Many do not wish to take sides. They do not try to stop the hostilities, believing that others will do it. Or, they may begin to take sides with whoever they believe will win, thereby causing an "uncivil war".

Where co-workers side with the bully, supporting the bully in her or his actions, or dumping on a target after s/he is gone, the problem of "identification with the aggressor" may be at play, much as it is with those who collaborate with the most diabolical generals during wartime or who become traitors. Erik Erison (1963) outlined this problem in his famous work, Childhood and Society, "the process of identification occurs when one person forms an emotional bond with another. Introjection then takes place, whereby identifying parties modify their own personalities and physical characteristics in an attempt to imitate the person they are identifying with" (Melsky, August, 2004).

Namie and Namie (2003:87) say that this theory may explain "how the target's best friend or the person who once stood as the target's strongest ally can turn against her". They suggest that other employees may not even be consciously aware of their behavior, or the devastating impact of it on the person being targeted. Or perhaps they prefer not to think about it.

Both management and co-worker inaction featured prominently in another story of psychological harassment, this time in the educational sector.

Anne was also a long standing employee who had held several posts in the organization, from teaching to management level assignments. She was highly committed to, and excelled at her work. She was loyal to the organization, producing consistently high quality results, and winning several awards for her efforts. For her, things changed with a new hire in her department – one she initially supported.

Anne was sympathetic to Marie's complaints about her last employer, and the alleged "old boy's club" that kept her from being able to contribute positively there. She gave her the benefit of the doubt, and supported her when Marie's students at first gave her negative feedback on her performance. She was impressed with Marie's commitment to social justice, and to the furtherance of human rights, especially in the workplace.

Anne learned too late, that Marie's words did not always align with her actions, and that Marie's ostensible commitment to human rights was not always universal. It seemed that for Marie, human rights applied more to "underdogs" than to those she considered to be "the enemy", in this case, her co-worker, Anne.

Claiming to have a commitment to anti-oppression or human rights work does not guarantee that the person making the claim will not engage in psychological warfare against those who do not hold her or his views, or who get in the way of their career path. More important than words, are the manner in which employees treat one another, whether they are able to function as team members or whether they attack team members with whom they disagree, or who are perceived to stand in the way of career advancement.

An excellent curriculum vitae, well written cover letter, and the ability to ace her only job interview with the institution landed Marie a job as a full-time faculty member. Anne was pleased at her hiring because she thought that Marie brought significant expertise in a specialized area. Anne encouraged Marie to share this expertise with the rest of the faculty team at meetings.

She also began to groom Marie to take over a specialized program, and gave her considerable responsibility while she was on vacation. But a few months after Marie's hiring, Anne began to notice that work was not getting done and results were not forthcoming. Work that others could do in an afternoon appeared to take Marie days, weeks, or months. Marie's promises seemed almost never to pan out.

Anne grew concerned that Marie may have also brought some baggage with her from her previous employer. She wondered if Marie had attempted to set her up to fight a battle for her with someone from her previous workplace. When confronted, Marie denied that she had a problem with this former co-worker about whom she had complained to Anne previously. This ran contrary to the former co-worker's assertions that Marie had been a problem in her previous workplace, and it ran counter to Marie's own criticisms of this individual in the recent past. Something was not quite adding up.

This is often how employers begin to identify concerns about those who may be bullying others – when work is not getting done, or promises are not being kept. It is often those who perform poorly who bully others who are more successful employees, in order to draw attention away from themselves. Sometimes the bully's view of her or himself far outstrips their ability to perform competently. An inflated sense of entitlement can add to the problem when the bully believes that he or she ought to be getting promotions and recognition for what amounts to very poor performance. Some have learned that by causing bosses and other employees to focus on someone they are targeting, they can often remain "under the radar" with respect to their own poor performance.

When correspondence that Marie wrote to important stakeholders was so poorly written that it reflected badly on the program that Anne had created, and on the department and institution, Anne confronted Marie again. But Marie appeared not to comprehend the seriousness of what had occurred. This was also odd, since Marie had, on other occasions, demonstrated an almost superior intelligence in Anne's view.

Finally, Anne felt she had no choice but to go to her supervisor out of concern for the reputation of the program, especially after it appeared that Marie was also getting politically enmeshed in the business of an external stakeholder organization important to the program.

What some would argue is a kind of "overinvolvement" in work, or a keen desire to see things "done right" is often a set up for workplace bullying. What a target may see as trying to do a job well, a potential bully will see as a threat. Feeling threatened, a bully will often launch a surprise attack, and this is what happened in Anne's case. This creates a kind of 'crazymaking' scenario for those, like Anne, who are high achievers. Do they downplay their talents and de-emphasize concerns about poor work performance by co-workers or direct reports in an effort to avoid dissension or possible bullying? This runs counter to what most employees are told by their employers – that if they work hard and achieve good results, they will be rewarded. Too often, as we see in this case, the "reward" may end up being an attack by a workplace bully who feels threatened or is envious of the high achiever's position in the organization.

> *Anne's supervisor interviewed Marie, and things apparently did not go well. He made the decision to end her association with the new program while allowing her to remain employed elsewhere in the department. From that moment on, after delivering a verbal threat that things would not end there, Marie launched a campaign of personal harassment against Anne that lasted for months, until Anne resigned her position, took a pay cut, and transferred out of the department.*

Of course, this was devastating for Anne, since her whole idea of what constituted fairness in the workplace was destroyed, and her sense of professional "safety" was shattered. This parallels what often happens to victims of crime or domestic violence when they first realize that their sense of safety is a myth.

> *Anne tried several times to get her supervisor to deal with the situation, but was ignored. Voice mails and e-mails were unreturned and her boss was AWOL much of the time. After many years of excellent service to the department, Anne was left entirely on her own in attempting to deal with Marie's campaign of harassment. She felt extremely hurt and betrayed by her supervisor and by the organization.*

It is often the sense of betrayal felt by conscientious workers when no one - no co-workers or supervisors, come to their aid that is the most harmful to their mental health. People who they thought were their friends appear to abandon them, not wishing to also be painted by the "victim" brush. It is as if they have developed a communicable disease. Victims of crime also describe this "shunning" phenomenon.

As much as it was Marie's actions that contributed to Anne leaving, it was also her immediate supervisor's refusal to establish a psychologically safe workplace that resulted in her decision to transfer.

Marie's campaign against Anne consisted of classic battle tactics – false accusations intended to undermine or destroy Anne's reputation; spying by hanging around the reception desk and listening to incoming phone calls that were directed to Anne; setting traps intended to cause Anne to make a mistake; drawing attention to even the smallest mistake; lying by denying that she had orchestrated phony issues when, in fact, she had, in an effort to embarrass Anne at staff meetings; threatening Anne and her supervisor through a third party; and finally, on Anne's last day in the department, following her into the ladies room and shouting accusations at her through the closed door of a toilet cubicle. This was afterwards referred to by Anne as "the bathroom attack", once she had regained her sense of humor. Many of these kinds of attacks and accusations occurred in private, with Marie then denying them publicly and instead attempting to portray herself as the victim of Anne's attacks on her.

Anne, having recently lost three members of her family, and with her father also deathly ill, was uncharacteristically vulnerable. That is when Marie chose to attack.

Just as what happened to Sue in the previous scenario, the bully in Anne's workplace appeared to target her for attack when she was at her most vulnerable.

As previously discussed, Anne's repeated requests for assistance from her manager went unanswered. She found that pushing back did not help, it only escalated Marie's behavior. Marie seemed to thrive on conflict, and bragged about other conflicts that she was also involved in with other individuals or organizations.

This parallels Sue's situation, where Anne felt that there was no way of effectively addressing getting out of a campaign of harassment of which she wanted no part. No matter what she thought of doing, she felt it would only make things worse.

Anne, feeling hurt, exhausted, and betrayed by an organization that once celebrated her significant accomplishments, later took a leave, to give herself time to plan her early retirement. The organization in which she had worked, and to which she had contributed so strongly for so many years, had utterly failed to assist her. Meanwhile, Marie remained safely ensconced in her position and nothing was done.

Like Sue, Anne also began plotting her escape from an organization that failed to defend her in spite of her many years of positive contributions. Once again, as in the previous example, an organization would lose the goodwill of someone who had significant expertise, had brought considerable prestige to it, and who had skills that the organization badly needed.

Anne found that in the aftermath of this campaign of harassment by Marie, that she was having difficulty sleeping, had gained weight, and often felt depressed and somewhat disoriented. At times she felt isolated, alone, and trapped. She began seeing a therapist who helped her to regain her perspective.

It was not until she began to research what had happened to her that she discovered that, like so many others, she had been the target of a campaign of psychological warfare by Marie, who had apparently had lots of practice using similar tactics against co-workers at her last place of employment. In both her current and previous workplaces, Marie tried to portray herself as the victim.

Anne had never had a complaint lodged against her by anyone, but had, nevertheless, had to resign from her position, take a pay cut, and transfer out of her department to put an end to Marie's harassment. Marie, on the other hand, had lost nothing.

Psychological warriors are not uncommon in modern workplaces They can be charming and convincing, and tend to be believable liars, but unfortunately do not possess the professional skills, or even the common human emotions that others do - emotions that could act as braking mechanisms on their anti-social and psychologically harmful behavior. Fear, remorse, and empathy are literally lacking

Marie had no empathy whatsoever for Anne. Anne described Marie as "having ice water flowing in her veins".

What allowed Marie to treat Anne as she did was her apparent demonization, and resulting dehumanization of her. Some authors have suggested that this is part of a tendency to paint targets as "immoral or untrustworthy, making the targets more deserving of such treatment" in their minds (Geffner, Braverman, Galasso & Marsh, 2004:84).

Marie may also have repeatedly set up conflict in an attempt to prove her dominance. "..aggressive individuals interpret interactions with others as contests to establish dominance…. Thus, aggressive people may believe that behaving in a hostile manner is an act of strength or bravery that gains respect from others and that not acting aggressively shows weakness and invites others to take advantage of them" (Geffner, Braverman, Galasso & Marsh, 2004; Anderson, 1994; Baron & Richardson, 1994). In this way, their aggression is seen as a way to "restore respect", in a classic win-lose move, rather than examining other ways of solving conflict situations. Of course, this type of "problem solving" leads to further problems since the person who "lost" is seldom willing to completely let it go, and it may come back to haunt the aggressor in the future.

In this case Marie refused to accept any responsibility for her own lack of performance, and instead blamed Anne, and projected her anger onto her. She saw Anne as the cause of all of her problems. Bies and Tripp (2005) have suggested that "an act of revenge is a response to certain situations in organizations that involve goal obstruction", and that appears to have been the case in this scenario. Marie may have believed that Anne's attempts to do her job well were obstructing her own chances of advancement.

Targets are seen as less than human and deserving of psychological attack by perpetrators. Unless stopped by those in positions of authority, these psychological mercenaries will go on to attack elsewhere in the same organization, in other organizations or venues, or they will move on to new positions, usually with letters of reference intact, where they will, in short order, find a new set of targets.

Managers are often hesitant to take action against these kinds of aggressors because they are particularly good at manipulating and even threatening superiors. Often managers attempt to ignore the problem in the hope that it will disappear. Unfortunately, that is almost never the case. What often occurs is that suddenly people in the department, usually the hardest workers, begin to retire early, take leaves, step down from their positions, or quit. Eventually the problem catches up with managers, especially when it leads to the loss of their best performers, but by then it has usually taken on much more serious implications.

Managers have sometimes found themselves in prolonged litigation, or the subject of attacks when they have failed to deal effectively with the "Maries" in their workplaces early on.

Some workplace bullies, trying a novel but effective tactic, will attempt to portray themselves as the victims of the target as Marie did. In fact, some may even be convinced that it is they who are the victims. Some authors have pointed out that "aggressive individuals ......have a propensity to implicitly believe that they are victims of exploitation or oppression by powerful others. These beliefs guide a confirmatory search for evidence supporting the idea that they are being victimized, which is used to justify their acts of aggression as legitimate strikes against oppression" (Averill, 1993; Finnegan, 1997; Tedeschi & Nesler, 1993, Toch, 1993).

A good way to determine truth from fiction in these instances is to examine actions rather than words, and an employee's actual performance over time, rather than any empty claims that an employee might make. It is the target who has usually lost something concrete – a job, a promotion, a leave, a particular honor, or taken a cut in salary. Targets have often taken pay cuts, been forced to transfer, take sick leave, long term disability, retire early, or have lost their jobs while those who tormented them have lost nothing and have perhaps gained in the exchange.

Bullies' abilities to lie convincingly will often cause them to be believed, and result in even more negative consequences for their hurt, depressed, or angry targets unless managers examine carefully who won and who lost in a particular conflict, and what an employee's **actual**, not **stated** record of achievement has been.

HOW COMMON IS WORKPLACE WARFARE?

Warren Shepell Consulting documented a 30% increase in reported cases of psychological harassment between 2003 and 2004. Rod Phillips, President and CEO of Warren Sheppell said: "If we're seeing that kind of increase, it suggests either it's on the increase or a combination of it's on the increase and people are becoming more open to disclosing it, ...We can't really put exact numbers around which is which, but we certainly see a higher level of activity around it" (Human Resources Professionals Association of Ontario, 2007).

Pizzino (2002) reports in a study of Canadian public employees, 69% of respondents said they were subjected to verbal aggression at work.

According to the Canadian Association of University Teachers, "an International Labour Organization (ILO) survey ranked Canada 4rth for workplace aggression, and it is perceived by Canadians as an important workplace issue".

In February of 2006, the Ontario English Catholic Teachers Association stated that "55% of the teacher and education workers in Ontario's public and Catholic systems have been bullied, either by someone in a superior position, by a colleague, by a parent or guardian, or by a student. Another 12% of teachers have not been bullied themselves but have witnessed bullying of others". This report was conducted on behalf of the Elementary Teachers' Association, the Ontario Secondary School Teachers' Federation, and the Ontario English Catholic Teachers' Association, that collectively represent 155,000 teachers and education workers in Ontario.

A report prepared by the National Injury Prevention Research Council (IPRC) estimates that two million Americans a year are also victims of workplace violence (IPRC, 2001). These kinds of serious incidents are on the increase across the U.S.

A large international study of more than 1800 HR and finance professionals in eleven countries "has revealed that one in four work in an office where bullying has taken place" (Employers' Law, June 7, 2006). The same study found that bullying is "far more common in firms with more than 100 staff".

In the UK, "a survey of more than 3500 staff revealed that more than two thirds of employees had been bullied at work, with women taking the brunt of bullying behavior. (Personnel Today, May 25, 2006). "

Workplace harassment can escalate into violence. Worker on worker homicide accounts for 7% of deaths (IPRC, 2001:9), and customer/client homicide accounts for up to 30% of deaths (National Institute for Occupational Safety, 2005).

Warfare in the workplace appears to be on the increase across the world, and may be reaching epidemic proportions. It is extremely injurious to individuals, their families, and organizations.

There are actions that heads of organizations can take to reduce or end this kind of behavior, but there must be the will to accomplish this. In light of the often serious repercussions caused by individuals who turn their workplaces into battlefields, it is critical that intervention occur early, be well planned, and forceful. The following chapters contain information that can help both employees and managers to begin to confront this insidious workplace problem.

REFERENCES

Anderson, F. (1994). The code of the streets. *Atlantic Monthly*, 273, 81-94.

Averill, J.R. (1993). Illusions of anger. In R.B. Felson & J.T, Tedeschi (Eds.), *Aggression and Violence: Social interactionist perspectives*. Washington, DC: American Psychological Association.

Adams, S.A. (1992). *Bullying at work - how to confront and overcome it.* London, UK: Virago Press.

Allcorn, S. (1994). *Anger in the workplace.* Westport, CT: Quorum Books.

Baron, R.A., Richardson, D.R. (1994). *Human Agression.* N.Y. Plenum.

Bassman, E.S. (1992). *Abuse in the Workplace - Management remedies and bottom line inpact.* Westport, CT: Quorum Books.

Belsey, B. (2008) *What can be done about cyberbullying?* Retrieved January 26, 2008 from: www.cyberbullying.ca

Bies, R.J., & Tripp, T.M. (2005) *The study of revenge in the workplace: Conceptual, ideological, and empirical issues.* In S. Fox & P.E. Spector (Eds) *Counterproductive Work Behavior: Investigations of Actors and Targets.* Washington, DC: American Psychological Association.

Bly, C. (1996). *Changing the bully who rules the world: Reading & thinking about ethics*, Minneapolis, MN: Milkweed Editions.

Canadian Centre for Occupational Health and Safety. (2006) *What is workplace bullying?* Retrieved August 17, 2007 from: www.ccohs. ca/oshanswers/psychosocial/bullying.html

CBC News. (October 10, 2002). *Cyber-bullying.* Retrieved August 20, 2007 from: www.cbc.ca/news/background/bullying/cyber_bullying.html

Davenport, N., Schwartz, D.R., & Elliott, G.P. (1999). *Mobbing - Emotional Abuse in the American Workplace.* Ames, Iowa: Civil Society Publishing.

Denenberg, R.V. & Braverman, M. (1999) *The Violence-prone workplace: A new approach to dealing with hostile, threatening, and uncivil behavior.* Ithaca, NY: Cornell University Press.

Field, T. (1006). *Bully in sight - how to predict, resist, challenge and combat workplace bullying.* UK: Success Unlimited.

Finnegan, W. (1997, December 1,). The Unwanted. *The New Yorker.* 61-78.

Geffnerr, R., Braverman, M., Galasso, J., Marsh, J., (2004) *Violence, Abuse and Harassment at Work and in Schools.* Binghampton, N.Y.: Haworth Press.

Human Resources Professional Association of Ontario. (2007). *Psychological harassment up this year in Canadian business.* Retrieved August 10, 2007 from: http://www.hrpao.org/HRPAO/ HRResourceCentre/KnowledgeCentre/newscluster2/Psychologic al+Harassment+Up.htm

Ishmael, A. (1999). *Harassment, bullying and violence at work.* London, UK: The Industrial Society.

Johnston, J. (2000). The equal opportunity harasser. Part 1: Workplace bully. Retrieved July 21, 2007 from: http://www.workrelationships. com/site/articles/workplacebully.htm

Keashly, L. (1998) Emotional abuse in the workplace: Conceptual and empirical issues. *Journal of Emotional Abuse,* 1(1), pgs 85-117.

McCarthy, P., Sheehan, M & Wilkie, W. (1996). *Bullying from backyard to boardroom.* UK: Millennium Books.

Melsky, R.E. (August, 2004). Identification with the aggressor: How crime victims cope with trauma. FBI Law Enforcement Bulletin. Retrieved January 10, 2007 from: http://www.findarticles.com/p/ articles/mi_m2194/is_8_73/ai_n6358315

Meyers, L. (2006, July& August). Office bullies. *Monitor on Psychology,* 37(7). American Psychological Association.

Milgram, S. (1974). *Obedience to authority; An experimental view.* NY: HarperCollins.

Namie, R. (1998). *Bully proof yourself at work!* Work Doctor. http:// www.workdoctor.com/

Namie, G. & Namie, R. (2000). *The bully at work.* Naperville, Ill: Sourcebooks, Inc

Nicarthy, G., Gottlieb, N. & Coffman, S. (1993). *You don't have to take it!* Emeryville, CA: Seal Press.

Peters, T., & Waterman, R.H. (1982). *In search of excellence: Lessons from America's best run companies.* NY: HarperCollins.

Pizzino, A. (2002). *Dealing with violence in the workplace: The experience of Canadian Unions.* In M. Gill, B. Fisher & V. Bowie (Eds) *Violence at work: Causes, patterns and preventio.* (pp. 168-179). Callompton, U.K.: Willan.

Randall, P. (1997) *Adult Bullying - Perpetrators and Victims.* Oxford, UK: Routledge.

Tedeschi, J.T., Nesler, M.S. (1993). *Grievances: Development and Reactions*: In R.B. Felson & J.T. Tedeschi (Eds), *Aggression and violence: Social interactionist perspectives.* Washington, DC: American Psychological Association.

Toch, H. (1993). *Violent men: An inquiry into the psychology of violence.* Washington, D.C., American Psychological Association.

Workplace Bullying and Trauma Institute. (2006). Washington, D.C. Retrieved July 21, 2007 from: http://bullyinginstitute.org/bbstudies/def.html

Wyatt, J. & Hare, C. (1997). *Work Abuse - How to recognize and survive it.* Rochester VT: Schenkman Books.

Zimbardo, P. G. (1971). The power and pathology of imprisonment. *Congressional Record.* (Serial No. 15, 1971-10-25). Hearings before Subcommittee No. 3, of the Committee on the Judiciary, House of Representatives, Ninety-Second Congress, *First Session on Corrections, Part II, Prisons, Prison Reform and Prisoner's Rights: California.* Washington, DC: U.S. Government Printing Office.

Zimbardo, P.G. (2007). *The Lucifer effect: Understanding how good people turn evil.* Retrieved July 22, 2007 from: http://www.lucifereffect.com/

CHAPTER TWO

Who are the workplace harassers and bullies?

Who are the workplace bullies and what motivates them? Targets often ask the question "why is he or she doing this?" or "why is this happening to me?" There is conflicting information in the literature about who the usual bullies are – co-workers, bosses or clients/ customers.

Spector & Fox (2006:29)) say that motivation depends upon whether the aggressive acts are "hot" or "cold". "Hot" or "affective" aggression refers to a situation where the primary goal is to psychologically injure the target, whereas "cold" or "instrumental" aggression is more calculated and the primary goal is a "means to a desired end". Hot aggression tends to be impulsive, cold aggression more carefully thought out.

According to Rod Phillips, president and CEO of WarrenShepell, "more than 40 per cent of bullying is colleague to colleague, while nearly 20 per cent of bullies are bosses. The National Institute for Occupational Safety and Health (July 28, 2004) also found that most bullying is co-worker to co-worker.

However, Namie (2003:4) found that 71% of workplace bullies "outrank their targets". This would suggest, as Namie does, that "most bullies are bosses". He says that this is often the case in workplaces where "competition is the name of the game" and individuals tend to gain personally at the expense of other employees.

The Commission des norms du travail in Quebec also found that some employees may harass their superiors, and the "persons involved may be individuals or a group of persons" (Commission des norms du travail, 2005:4). Customers may also be involved.

Therefore managers may also be victims, especially middle managers. "A report from the Chartered Management Institute (CMI), *Bullying at work: the experience of managers*, reveals that 39% of all managers have been bullied in the past three years. Almost half the middle managers (49%) said they had been victims of bullying (Personnel Today, September 20, 2005).

Workplace bullies are just as likely to be female as male, and they cross all industries and socio-economic statuses. The harassment can be verbal or psychological abuse" (Talbot, 2004).

The conclusion that can be drawn from these studies is that anyone, at any level of the organization, can become a target of a workplace bully.

The Canada Safety Council (2007) sees workplace bullying as a "grab for control by an insecure, inadequate person, an exercise of power through humiliation of the target". These are individuals with "poor or non-existent social skills and little empathy." Feeling not quite up to the task of fulfilling their professional obligations, they "[seethe] with resentment, bitterness, hatred and anger [and are] driven by jealousy and envy" (U.K National Bullying Advice Line, 2006).

Whatever the reason people psychologically harass others in the workplace, whether for personal advantage, or to exert control, there are definite categories of bullies.

The Competitive Bully

Some workplace bullies are competitive, drawn to a particularly cutthroat workplace culture. They see bullying as a way to get to the top by trying to usurp their victim's position. These individuals are similar to their counterparts in the criminal world who strike when they see vulnerability – an opportunity. Their goal is to take something important for themselves from their targets – a job, a reputation, money, prestige. They tend to be jealous and envious of other's successes, believing it is s/he who should be rewarded, not someone else. In many cases their ambitions far outstrip their actual abilities, but this does not stop them from seeking control and the limelight.

Competitive bullies do not to want to get caught, because that would interfere with their ambitions, so they may engage in passive-aggressive behavior. They can be quite charming in public, preferring to torment their targets in private where there are no witnesses.

Once confronted, they tend to deny their actions, sometimes quite vigorously, and set up "she said, he said" scenarios that make i difficult for those in positions of authority to determine what actually occurred and take appropriate action.

Their methods tend to be "stealthy". They may engage in sabotage of another's belongings, feed misinformation to their intended victim to try to set them up to fail, place them in an information vacuum, making it impossible for them to do their jobs, they may try to create problems and blame them on the victim, or post cruel messages on anonymous websites. They may also try to work through others using lies and innuendo to damage someone's reputation, so that the true cause of a target's discomfort is difficult to discern.

Their passive-aggressive tactics and failure to follow through when they take on tasks may turn work teams into battle zones. "Divide and conquer" tactics may add to the problem.

Marie, described in an earlier chapter, was a competitive bully. Seeing a vulnerable target, because of Anne's preoccupation with recent tragedies in her life, and wanting both revenge and an opportunity for advancement, Marie struck, with attacks on her target's reputation, self concept, and sense of self worth. Her attempts to devalue her in front of her own team succeeded to some extent. Her lies and deception stood her in good stead with her boss, who never took action to stop her. Her behavior usually occurred in private. When Anne spoke to her, she would shun her, turning her back on her and refusing to answer, in an attempt to provoke her. She would sit at the back in staff meetings, with Anne at the front, and stare at her, or smirk whenever Anne spoke. She withheld information from Anne, making it difficult for Anne to do her job, and failed to follow through on tasks that Anne asked her to do.

In the end, she successfully drove Anne, a respected and longstanding employee, from her position. No doubt feeling victorious and powerful, she indicated an interest in Anne's job. When that did not succeed, she decided next to try her hand in the political arena, where she was also unsuccessful.

Interestingly, Anne, in contrast, although bearing some scars from her encounter with Marie, was able to use her resilience and resourcefulness to continue a successful consulting and teaching career. She was able to build a small business where she could invest her talents, and used her writing skills to produce books and manuals that other professionals found useful and that sold well.

The Openly Hostile Bully

Individuals who make no attempts to cover up their bullying tactics fall into the category of hostile bullies. Their goal is to rule the workplace through fear, causing everyone to do their bidding or risk their wrath. They want absolute control, but often have no idea of what to do with it. Lacking vision, they may focus on numbers and demand performance from others, while being unable to accept criticism or even disagreement themselves. They may criticize someone's performance in front of their peers, call people names, complain about co-workers and direct reports, belittle employees in public and private. Often they subject people to biting sarcasm and put downs.

These workplace warriors are driven to hurt others by overwhelming feelings of personal inadequacy, in a desperate attempt to elevate their own positions. Anger is experienced as a core emotion. Driven by their constant feelings of inadequacy, and at times, fears of abandonment, they have learned that the best defense against these feelings is to attack and attempt to control others, especially those who cannot or will not fight back. The parallels to what occurs in domestic violence situations are unmistakable, and point to dependent personalities, fearful that losing control over others will lead to their own ruin.

Some openly hostile bullies thrive on conflict, and seek to create it wherever they go. Others collapse when confronted, their inflated false selves crashing to the ground.

Some of these individuals may have mental health conditions called personality disorders leaving them unable to regulate their emotions and moods. But more often than not, they are neurotic people who struggle with internal feelings of insecurity.

Sometimes openly hostile bullies combine their verbal assaults with other forms of harassment like withholding information necessary for someone to do her or his job, or they may put someone in an information vacuum, or remove privileges or even basic necessities from them as a form of punishment intended to cause hurt and humiliation.

> *Larry worked in the entertainment industry for a family member who fit the description of an openly hostile bully. For years Larry felt forced to put up with conduct that was verbally abusive, offensive, and sometimes racist.*

> *The family member, Sue, displayed behavior that alternated between being encouraging to being damaging and insulting. This created a "crazy making" situation for Larry who never knew what he would encounter on any given day.*

> *Larry worked for years in a situation where he never knew if Sue would issue purchase orders needed for him to do his job. He did not know if she would even speak to him, since he once got the silent treatment for two months.*

> *At other times he was subjected to insults and blame, and he heard Sue call other suppliers, clients, and competitors "assholes" or "idiots".*

> *His request for time off was denied. He was denied projects that he requested to work on. He was never given enough money to do the job and was even asked to donate his air miles so that the President of the company could use them. He was told "what's the big deal?" when he refused. This type of treatment was not confined to Larry. Other employees were also made to look bad if they did not volunteer their time and expertise.*

Providing work for free is often an expectation of an openly hostile bully. Exploitation of employees is commonplace, with the bullies rationalizing their behavior by suggesting that people need to "pay their dues" if they want promotions.

> *Larry was always told that if he was not happy he should move on, but when he decided to do that he was bribed back with a large pay raise.*

This type of bully requires a victim in order to feel better about her or himself. It should not be surprising that Sue would lure Larry back. Without him as her "whipping boy", her own feelings of insecurity threatened to overwhelm her.

> *In a classic projection, Sue told Larry that he had a bad attitude and could not get along with others, and that no one wanted to work with him, when in fact, these statements pertained more to Sue than to him. The very next day, Sue told him he was doing a great job.*

The tendency to project the bully's personal inadequacies onto others is commonplace. Feeling anxious and overwhelmed with self-criticism, bullies seek to "offload" some of their bad feelings onto others. Projection of their own characteristics onto another person is a way to achieve this.

> *Sue surrounded herself with "yes men" who she then foisted onto other employees, including Larry. This also made it difficult for him to do his job.*

Since openly hostile bullies have such fragile egos, they cannot accept the presence of anyone who might challenge or disagree with them. The presence of individuals who will curry favor or "suck up" is critical to their own self image. Hence openly hostile bullies will often surround themselves with people who will agree with them irrespective of how wrong their decisions may be.

> *Larry was given impossible deadlines, and continuously set up for failure. Promised public recognition for his work at a Christmas party never materialized. When he reacted to this mistreatment he was told that he was bitter and too emotional, in another glaring example of a projection by Sue.*

> *The only way that Larry could cope with the situation was to seek therapy. He was left with little self-esteem or self-confidence after years of this kind of treatment, and continues to bear the scars.*

> *It was only when Sue's behavior began to negatively impact Larry's daughter and family relationship that he decided to call it quits. Looking back, he realizes that he should have left a lot sooner, but stayed in part because his boss was "family" and*

because he either needed the money, or was lured back by raises or more promises.

In many ways Larry's situation also paralleled what happens in cases of domestic violence, where the perpetrator is abusive, but can also be very charming and kind in a "cycle of abuse". This confuses the perpetrator's victims and may greatly extend the period of time that someone continues to be victimized, always believing that things will change for the better.

Sue's abusive and erratic behavior created a workplace war zone, complete with the occupational hazards that often accompany this kind of psychological abuse.

Openly hostile bullies like Sue are commonplace in all kinds of companies, agencies, and organizations. They cause their employees to live in fear of them. Because employees' economic livelihoods or pensions depend upon staying in their jobs, they may suffer irreparable harm, or exhibit post traumatic stress symptoms. This is a very high price to pay to earn a living.

Openly hostile bullies are unlikely to ever accept responsibility for the impact of their behavior on others. Lacking empathy, they are more likely to blame the victim for her or his own psychological injuries. In some cases, they will use their power, as occurred in Larry's case, to even turn other family members against the target.

The Self Absorbed Bully

Some perpetrators are simply extremely self absorbed and apparently truly unaware of the impact of their actions on others. Narcissistic, utterly bereft of self-awareness, they have no idea how their words and actions may hurt other people. These individuals tend to focus entirely on their own personal needs to the exclusion of others' needs or feelings. To them, others are merely a means to an end, and have value only for what use they are to the bully. These are the individuals who, when in conversation with others, constantly return the conversation to themselves and what they want to say. They have to be the centre of attention, and will speak endlessly about the minutiae of their lives, simply assuming that everyone is as interested in what they are saying as they are.

Everything is all about them.

These individuals tend to bully by completely ignoring the needs and feelings of others, causing them to feel unimportant and undervalued. They make insensitive comments that are hurtful, and fail to apologize, or even understand when an apology is required.

They may attempt to make themselves look important by taking credit for others' work, and are seldom able to provide positive reinforcement to co-workers or to direct reports except where it might benefit them to do so. They are the centre of their own universe and for them others barely exist, except as "servants". Also known as "users", they tend not to have evil intent, and do not actively seek to harm others unless thwarted or "crossed", but do so out of ignorance of others' needs and feelings. Self absorbed or narcissistic bullies do enormous harm through their neglect, always taking, but giving little or nothing in return. They tend to leave a swath of anger, frustration and feelings of betrayal in their wake.

> *Janet worked for a self absorbed bully for years before she could finally stand it no more. Good at her job, she took on a great deal more than was necessary, and did so because she liked her boss, Joe.*

> *Joe was a free spirit, always out and about in his fancy car. While he had some management ability, rather than do his job, he much preferred to drive the ladies around, or go to nice coffee shops and restaurants. Joe liked the good life and constantly bragged about his lifestyle, his trophy wife, his children. The life he described was, of course, different from reality, but that did not stop Joe from talking about how rich, successful, or privileged he and his family were. He would regularly brag about minutiae in his life, simply assuming that everyone had an interest in his projects, his children, his material goods, his wife's job and ambitions, his cars, the restaurants he went to, and every other aspect of his life.*

This kind of behavior is not uncommon for self-absorbed bullies. They have no interest whatsoever in other people's feelings, opinions, or lives, but they may feign interest for awhile, just to keep the other person involved enough that they can continue to use them as "listening posts". Sometimes they will flatter others in an effort to get them to do their work for them, thereby allowing them to spend more time on activities that interest them.

Joe's "talent" was in finding good, hardworking staff, especially highly competent women, who would do much of his work for him, thereby leaving him free to pursue his lifestyle.

The problems began when some of these women quit, took demotions and transferred out, or took extended leaves. Fed up with not receiving promotions, raises, or even recognition for their work, and getting little or no support to do their jobs, because of Joe's frequent absences and unwillingness to make decisions, they decided to stop working for him. Joe's reaction when this happened was surprise. Apparently completely unaware of the impact of his behavior on his "team", Joe resented them for abandoning him.

This is another characteristic of self absorbed bullies. Having no understanding of how their callousness and lack of concern for others affects those around them, they may see themselves as being victimized when others finally leave them, unable to stand their neglect any longer.

Feeling the pressure created by their leaving, Joe quickly set about to find other women to replace them and take on the headaches that Joe had created because of his neglect. This left him free to carry on business as usual – out of sight, out of mind. While Joe was out and about, the highly competent women in his department worked long hours and kept the department running, all the time hoping for promotions, or at least acceptance, until, feeling overwhelmed, some of them either stepped down from their positions or quit altogether.

Joe never actually "got it" about why his staff were burning out, going on stress leave, seeking transfers out of his area, or quitting. He thought he was a great boss and had no idea what all these people were whining about. In fact, he would sometimes characterize their requests for assistance, or even that he make decisions to support them in their work, as whining. Adding sexism to injury, it was no wonder that highly competent and conscientious women in his area were stepping down from their positions, or leaving. Nevertheless Joe blithely continued to blame them, and even punished some of them by removing basic amenities like permanent desks and chairs, never recognizing that it was his lack of investment of time, energy, or concern that was causing the problem.

Janet, who had worked so hard for years, and had been dedicated to Joe and to her job, was left with nothing much to show for her hard work – no promotions, not even acceptance. She finally took a lateral promotion out of Joe's department in disgust and was later promoted again by a manager who recognized her hard work, dedication, and talent.

Predictably, she never heard from Joe again. Meanwhile, Joe enjoyed the protection of other senior male managers in the "old boy's club". Nothing was done to curb his obvious callousness and irresponsible and sometimes unethical behavior, and he was left free to pursue his extra curricular activities, and collect a good salary while others did his job for him.

Janet, feeling hurt, used and betrayed was left to pick up the pieces of her encounter with Joe. She described herself as "feeling stupid" that she had been taken in by his charm, and said that she should have recognized what was happening years ago.

Some lessons are very hard ones to learn.

Self absorbed bullies like Joe often get away with murder. Charming and convincing, they use their likeability to manipulate their way through life, finding unsuspecting people to do their bidding, who are taken with their charm and believability, even when they lie and exploit them. There appears to be no shortage of willing victims. Even those who are aware of the track record of bullies like Joe may still believe that things will be different for them. They can be seen attempting flattery, and chatting up the narcissistic boss, believing it will help them in their careers. They often learn too late that it is they who are being exploited, and they end up leaving bitter, frustrated and angry at being used for so long.

The "Joes" of the world live what appear to be externally comfortable lives, but their relationships are often in shambles. Eventually, those they have duped get wise, and leave them, or come to feel nothing but disrespect and contempt for them. They are then left scratching their heads and feeling like they are the victims of others' betrayals, with not a hint of understanding of how they have contributed to their own relationship problems. Self absorbed bullies simply do not take responsibility. Denial is a way of life. They blithely coast through their lives and careers on the backs of others, leaving a trail of people who feel hurt and used behind them.

Bullies With Addictive Personalities

Some perpetrators are bullies who lack the rationality to recognize what they are doing to others. Those who abuse drugs or alcohol, or engage in problem eating, gambling, or sex may bring unhealthy interpersonal and family dynamics into the workplace. Their continued functioning thrives on secrecy, enabling, and cover-up. Their addictions rule their lives, and unfortunately, when they enter the workplace, the lives of others as well.

These bullies may show up for work impaired, or not show up at all, and believe it is the responsibility of others to cover for them, or help them appear to still be able to do their jobs. They demand enabling behavior of anyone who reports to them, or over whom they have control, thereby placing their employees in dicey ethical and legal situations.

Their goal is to offload responsibility for their addictions onto others. These bullies control through manipulation. They may lie with impunity, and attempt to be charming to get others to "help them out". When others refuse to do this, they may witness the more abusive side of this type of bully. Targets may be berated by them, or even physically threatened. This type of perpetrator's behavior may become irrational and appear out of control, and cause fear in co-workers, bosses, or direct reports.

Because addictions impair judgment, and often impulse control, these are among the most dangerous individuals in today's workplaces. They are the "time bombs" ticking away in the workplace, in danger of exploding given the right "trigger".

Just as in domestic violence, substance abuse can play a part in workplace violence. These are the bullies who, because of their impaired judgment and poor impulse control, may feel that they have nothing left to lose if they lose their jobs, or face disciplinary action, and are therefore more likely to take revenge on their co-workers or bosses.

Their tendency to use lies and manipulation as coping strategies makes these bullies very difficult to deal with. Highly emotionally volatile, they may strike out - sometimes without warning.

Because males who abuse substances are sometimes medicating against other mental health conditions, like depression or anxiety, and those with gambling addictions may be quite desperate, they may also pose a risk of suicide or homicide.

> Gerry was a substance abusing bully who worked in the military. He was often abusive to his staff, was crude to women employees in particular, and generally socially inappropriate. After another manager attempted to blow the whistle on Gerry's totally inappropriate behavior and substance abuse, Gerry targeted him for "payback" by mercilessly harassing him. That manager later won a rather large settlement based on a psychological harassment claim. Unfortunately he also paid a high emotional price for fighting back.

Managers who realize that one of their employees may be under the influence of an addiction, need to act quickly to stop their abusive behavior and assist them to seek help. If they refuse, early action to end their employment is often the best option. The longer this kind of bully remains in a workplace, the more dangerous the situation often becomes for co-workers, supervisors, and for the bully her or himself.

The Thrill Seeking, Power Hungry Bully

Some simply enjoy the power they can exert over another, and prefer to play mind games, entertained by watching the negative effects of their actions on others. Their behavior is intended to feed their constant need for stimulation, and it helps to defend against feelings of personal insecurity or boredom.

These tend to be individuals who are highly intelligent, but who under perform, and who aim to disguise their personal flaws by bullying others who they see as more competent and respected. They are individuals who hurt and attack others to make themselves feel more powerful, and are likely to engage in unkind or spiteful behavior towards a target in private, then deny it in public or when called to account.

They enjoy bringing about the downfall of someone who they see as more powerful or capable than themselves. Ruining another's reputation or career brings them a sense of secondary power, achieved at the expense of the more powerful person they have sabotaged.

This type of individual requires ongoing stimulation, and may have a history of conflict with others in their private and professional lives. They will likely have dubious work and possibly school histories, and have often left behind them a trail of formerly competent co-workers or bosses who have become distrustful and paranoid, in some cases unable to perform their work to the same standard as before.

Because of the lies often spread by this kind of bully, their targets will experience self-doubt and feel isolated from possible sources of support. Their insidious attacks are highly damaging to their targets who may develop depression or other mental health problems as a result of their constant attacks and attempts to set them up. In extreme situations, the underhanded tactics of thrill seeking bullies have ended tragically in the emotional breakdown or suicides of their victims.

This kind of ongoing passive-aggressive interaction can seriously disrupt a workplace, causing conflict and confusion. These kinds of bullies like to work covertly, and often succeed when the target feels too embarrassed or ashamed to report their antisocial behavior (Personnel Today, November 7, 2006).

Clear signals that a workplace may be plagued by this kind of bully is when conflict suddenly flares up on a team after someone's transfer in, or the hiring of someone new, especially where a team has worked well together previously. Observable distress on the part of the "team leader" or "informal leader" or particularly competent employee, who is well respected, may be another symptom of the presence of this kind of bully.

Hillary was the clinical director in a mental health service for children. Having faced an uprising by staff in her previous position at another agency, she arrived at her new position with considerable paranoia, a sense of insecurity, and a strong need for control. She could not accept the views of anyone who disagreed with her and targeted direct reports as well as two particularly competent front line workers if they disagreed with her. Belittling their views and ability in staff meetings, she set out to destroy their professional credibility. She toyed with her direct reports for her own amusement, playing them off against each other.

She also played mind games with other professionals, mischaracterizing them or their work. She saved her strongest attacks for supervisors who reported to her, undermining them at every opportunity. When confronted on her behavior, loud arguments could be heard from behind her closed office door. She seemed to thrive on conflict.

When people began to quit, she left, ostensibly to go to graduate school to earn her doctorate. Eventually, however, that also went awry as she was found to have tampered with results of her research to support her hypothesis, and was subject to academic penalty.

Thrill seeking bullies like Hillary draw their sense of personal power from the humiliation and degradation they inflict on others. In need of a constant supply of adrenalin, they initiate conflict for the fun of it. By keeping everyone slightly off kilter, they feel safer and more in control.

Most people tend not to confront bullies like Hillary, fearful of consequences to their careers. This is exactly what bullies like Hillary bank on – that people will not fight back if they appear aggressive enough.

Thrill seeking bullies, like all the others, need to be stopped. Their negative divide and conquer behavior should be identified and addressed by those with the authority to do so. The longer a thrill seeking bully is allowed to operate freely, the more likely there will be distrust, infighting, backstabbing and resignations from a team

As in the other scenarios, organizations and individuals lose when thrill seeking bullies win.

The Psychopathic Bully

Unfortunately, in some cases, the problem may be more sinister. Dr. Robert Hare, an authority in the study of psychopathy and the developer of the Psychopathy Checklist-Revised (PCL-R) used throughout the criminal justice and mental health systems, says that "not all the criminals are in prison; some of them are in the boardroom."

Dr. Hare, quoted by John Worsley Simpson in the Financial Post (May 10, 2006) states: "Psychopaths are often exceptionally bright. They are cunning manipulators of people, and have no compunction about doing whatever they believe will bring them success or fame or satisfaction in their endeavors. They lie with facility and without the slightest pang of conscience. And the evidence seems to suggest they are born this way". Dr. Hare further states: "psychopaths account for only about 1 per cent of the general population. But ... there would be a higher proportion in such areas as business, politics, law enforcement agencies, law firms, religious organizations and yes, the media".

Psychopathic bullies tend to be drawn to the corridors of power. They will do whatever it takes to achieve personal gain. Other people do not exist as feeling entities for them since they lack feeling themselves, and generally also lack fear. Those with whom they work are often awestruck at their boldness. These are the Darwinistic predators of the workplace who live by a code of "survival of the fittest". To them, anyone who they exploit, manipulate or ruin are the authors of their own misfortune. Psychopathic bullies will often blame their victims for their own demise: "if she hadn't been so gullible, I couldn't have taken her job", or "if he wasn't so stupid, I couldn't have outmaneuvered him".

They have the ability to use charm to get what they want from others, but if that fails, lying, cheating, threatening, even physical violence, are not beyond the capabilities of a psychopathic bully. Their goal is to win at any cost. Those who get in their way are quickly "taken out" by whatever type of lie or manipulation is likely to work best. Unlike mere mortals, their lack of fear, remorse, or concern for others allows them to engage in damaging and underhanded behavior that most would never dream of. Reckless, they may squander profits, ruin programs and services and defraud organizations with impunity. Most of their victims are completely charmed by them, and never realize how much they have been used until it is too late (Babiak and Hare, 2006).

Because of their lack of boundaries or concern for others, psychopathic bullies also have no compunction about "sleeping their way to the top". They tend to find "patsies" who are needy, who they can manipulate and use as allies, and they will control these individuals with lies, promises, and even sexual liaisons in order to ensure their loyalty. Like other types of bullies, they may be male or female, but they tend, more often, to be male.

Because they enjoy power and control over others, psychopathic bullies are more likely to be senior managers, or have senior management aspirations. In studying this problem and commenting on it in his book, *Snakes in Suits*, Dr. Hare says: "we analyzed the succession plans of a few hundred North American executives and noted that the similarities between the developmental issues for some managers identified as 'high potentials' and psychopathic-like features were startling." The results of his study were of such concern that he and Dr. Paul Babiak developed the B-Scan 360 used by companies to scan for psychopathic traits in potential hires. In light of the harm that can be done to an organization by hiring someone in a senior position who has psychopathic traits, more and more companies and organizations are opting for the use of this tool.

Most psychopathic bullies are thought to be male, but in some cases, female psychopaths can be equally destructive in a workplace.

Amelia arrived at her position on the basis of her advanced degree from a highly reputable university. Of above average intelligence, and unbothered by failing to demonstrate by her actions the values and scruples to which she claimed to subscribe, she initiated a sexual relationship with the married head of the organization. Blithely unconcerned about the impact of her actions on her own husband and children and on his, she used her privileged position as the head's consort to maintain her senior management position, in spite of the havoc she wreaked in her department.

Grooming two or three informants, who spied on others and were willing to follow her direction, and who she protected in exchange for their loyalty, she ruled by fear, intimidation, and subtle threats.

She never hesitated to target other managers for sharp tongued rebuke in management meetings and never faced consequences for her behavior because of her special status with the head of the organization. If anything did not go her way, she simply used her leverage with him to get whatever she wanted.

Other managers were extremely resentful of her behavior and her special status, but all failed to challenge her for fear of committing professional suicide.

Her undermining and abuse of her staff and colleagues continued for years, but she survived repeated grievances, firings and resignations. No one could touch her until personal tragedy finally intervened to end her reign of terror. Once she was gone, the entire culture of her area changed as people finally felt safe to come out of their offices and restore the collegiality that had once existed there.

Where intense fear of reprisals exists in a workplace and people are constantly distrustful and "watching their backs", or "keeping their heads down", the presence of a psychopathic bully is almost guaranteed. People usually try to stay out of the way of this individual, but those who fail to do so, are often cut down quite mercilessly.

Psychopathic bullies present a real challenge for managers, especially since they are so adept at grooming "patsies" to support them. They may be well versed in flattering those to whom they report, or may even be using their sexuality to win their support as in Amelia's case.

Managers who try to act against a psychopathic bully need to have their ducks in a row. They need to have unshakeable evidence, and be willing to quickly take the necessary action to remove them from the workplace.

The "Personality-Disordered" Bully

Some workplace bullies tend to be individuals who have a history of contentious work, professional, and personal relationships and bullying behavior. Family relationships may be problematic, and these individuals may also have been involved in previous confrontations with other employers, with professional bodies, and/or educational institutions. In some more serious cases they will have had contact with the criminal justice system. These individuals are likely to have a mental illness, termed a personality disorder, which significantly disrupts their abilities to maintain healthy relationships over the long term. Poor impulse control, reckless disregard for others, poor emotional regulation, volatility, splitting, and passive-aggressive behavior are all symptoms of the kinds of mental health conditions that may create havoc in a workplace.

Some authors have suggested that some aggressive individuals may not have internalized the same cultural norms and values that define socially adaptive behavior, may respond in a more hostile manner, and have internalized biases that help them to rationalize aggressive behavior. These factors may be predictors of aggressive behavior (James, McIntyre, Glisson, Green, Patton, LeBreton, Frost, Russell, Sablynski, Mitchell & Williams, 2005).

People who are aggressive may see threat or "malevolent intent" in other people where others do not (Crick & Dodge, 1994).

Individuals who display the symptoms described in the DSM IV-TR under the label "borderline personality disorder" can also create havoc in a workplace. Marked by "a pervasive pattern of instability of interpersonal relationships, self-image, and affects, and marked impulsivity", individuals with this condition are said to experience "intense abandonment" fears. These are people who alternate between idealizing and despising others, believing that the other "does not care enough, does not give enough, is not there enough" (American Psychiatric Association, 2000:707). These individuals can "empathize with and nurture other people, but only with the expectation that the other person will be there in return to meet their own need on demand". In other words, every kind act has a string attached.

Some engage in a means of anxiety reduction called "splitting". Splitting refers to "a mental mechanism in which the self or others are reviewed as all good or all bad, with failure to integrate the positive and negative qualities of self and others into cohesive images. Often the person alternately idealizes and devalues the same person" (APA, 2000: 707). This can sometimes result in people on a team being played off against each other with some characterized as "all good" and others as "all bad".

These types of bullies demonize their targets and try to destroy their reputations or good names. They can be highly manipulative, flattering some of their co-workers, and appearing to be their friends, while attempting to destroy another co-worker at the same time. This kind of behavior can be very confusing to people in a workplace. They may have a hard time believing that someone who is so charming or nice to them might be capable of vicious attacks on someone else.

These are co-workers who everyone seems to want to avoid. Like substance abusing bullies they may bring attempts to cope that are no longer functional or adaptive into the workplace. Most have tragic personal histories of trauma, where they had to learn to cope in ways that seem toxic to others. For example, their tendency to play people off against each other can create chaos on a team, where everyone has a different opinion of the person with this condition, and may even argue over who is right about them. In families of origin that were violent, this type of strategy may have prevented the bully from being hurt, by drawing attention away from themselves and onto others. Frequently creating chaos in their immediate environment will also help them to avoid having to attend to internal demons that they experience as frightening.

It can be confusing to work with someone who has this condition since they may shift from being "a needy supplicant for help to a righteous avenger of past mistreatment" (APA,2000), and they may overreact to environmental stressors by frequently "expressing inappropriate, intense anger and difficulty controlling their anger".

In situations of extreme stress, this individual may also become quite paranoid, and project negative intent or attributions onto others in the workplace. After a serious blowup, a co-worker may be shocked when they greet them the next day as if nothing had ever happened. That is because people with this personality disorder lack emotional memory. They literally cannot remember the intensity of the blowup, and may wonder at the reaction they get. This, of course, further feeds their paranoia.

The ramifications of having to work with someone with this condition are obvious. The workplace is chaotic, with people walking on eggshells to avoid setting this person off. Most try to avoid having to deal with the person for fear that their impulsive and angry behavior could be turned on them, or that they will be falsely accused of some affront.

Some bullies may have an antisocial disorder rather than full blown psychopathy, but still have malevolent intent towards their targets (Namie & Namie, 2003), showing no remorse after having hurt or injured another person. This type of individual is likely to be extremely deceitful and a pathological liar. She or he can become quite aggressive, and behave impulsively, while refusing to accept any responsibility for her or his behavior. Individuals with this condition are unlikely to have any regard for the rights of others, and will feel quite fine about manipulating their co-workers, then blaming them for having been taken in. Workplaces where a bully with antisocial personality disorder is employed are often characterized by hurt, anger, blame, and feelings of betrayal.

Passive-aggressive bullies can also cause considerable disruption in a workplace. The Diagnostic and Statistical manual (American Psychiatric Association, 2000:789) of the American Psychiatric Association, in discussing Passive-Aggressive Personality Disorder, refers to "a pervasive pattern of negativistic attitudes and passive resistance to demands for adequate performance in social and occupational situations..." These individuals are said to "obstruct the efforts of others by failing to do their share of the work", and this obstruction is evidenced by "procrastination, forgetfulness, stubbornness, and intentional insufficiency especially in response to tasks assigned by authority figures"

Individuals with this condition are unlikely to accept responsibility for their underperformance or disruptive behavior, and will instead "complain of being misunderstood by others", while appearing "sullen and argumentative", "unreasonably criticizing and scorning authority", "expressing envy and resentment to those apparently more fortunate", persistently complaining of personal misfortune in an exaggerated fashion, and alternating between "hostile defiance and contrition" (APA, 2000:789).

Confusion and resentment reign in a workplace with a passive-aggressive bully. No one knows who to trust, and many will become alienated and attempt to avoid this kind of workplace altogether, fearful of being drawn into the negative politics of the place.

These are the bullies who are very good at playing the victim, even when it is they who have hurt someone. These are the individuals who will make complaints against their superiors for "harassment", when they are taken to task, when in fact, it is they who were not doing their jobs.

June worked for a school board and was, by all accounts an excellent teacher who became a department head. She tried very hard to run a good department characterized by social events, strong teamwork, and a commitment to excellence. All of this came crashing down for her when a new team member, Rosslyn, appeared unable to work as part of the team. If she did not get her way in every instance, Rosslyn caused messy situations or arguments. She seemed to be unable to take direction. In every office she had worked, she could not get along with others, the current situation being no exception. Others tended to try to avoid her, and she usually works in isolation.

When confronted by June about the necessity of adhering to particular rules or procedures in the department, Rosslyn accused June of "interfering". Rosslyn refused to teach the standard curriculum, and complained about her co-workers because they would not do things her way. She was unable to work with anyone, in spite of appearing "chipper" and being able to engage in banter with her students.

The constant insubordination and refusal to take direction took up hours and hours of June's time and threatened to destroy the team she had worked so hard to build.

When June would not simply give in to her every demand, Rosslyn filed a grievance against her. This created considerable anxiety for June even though she knew that her actions had not been unreasonable, and that she was just doing her job. In the end the mediator who was appointed to deal with the situation found in June's favor, saying that the situation "could not go on". Even after this outcome Rosslyn threatened to hire a lawyer and fight it, and remained extremely angry with June.

Rosslyn had obviously been in therapy since she regularly used "therapeutic language" that she threw back at June. She claimed to better understand brain development than June, but when June checked, it appeared that her information was incomplete or wrong. This raised concerns that perhaps Rosslyn's unwillingness to teach the curriculum occurred because she may not understand the material. Her attacks on June, an older, more experienced, and well respected teacher, may have been attempts to ruin her reputation in an effort to draw attention away from her own inadequacies.

The impact on June was considerable. She stopped running her department in the open and consultative way that she previously had, and became more guarded in her communication. She was very cautious around Rosslyn, constantly guarding against possible attacks. She began to have trouble sleeping, and the constant stress upset her family life. She found herself, along with other employees, constantly "walking on eggshells" tiptoeing around Rosslyn.

After many, many years of teaching, June has decided to retire. Once again, the educational system will lose an excellent teacher, while someone who cannot accept direction, and causes conflict wherever she goes continues in her teaching position.

Mental health issues in the workplace are now recognized as a serious concern. According to the Canadian Alliance on Mental Illness and Mental Health (2006), "in Ontario, 8% of the working population has a diagnosable mental disorder" and "mental illness accounts for 46% of all long term and short term disability claims"."Workplace absenteeism due to mental health problems accounted for 7.1% of total payroll".

Conflict Resolution Does Not Work

Namie & Namie (2003) point out that the usual rules of communication and conflict resolution cannot apply when dealing with workplace bullies, especially those with mental illness, because the "target" is usually "swept into the relationship involuntarily" and because "mutual benefit or gain is not the goal, control is, and the target wants none of it". The involuntary nature of the bully-target relationship negates the usual assumption that any conflict involves two people, both of whom have some responsibility for its outcome.

Conflict resolution can only be practiced in an environment where there is trust and a mutual agreement to try to work out the conflict (Cahn & Abigail, 2006). It cannot often be resolved where one individual has personal issues better discussed in a therapist's or psychiatrist's office.

Danger Signals

Some workplace bullies are potentially violent, and employers need to be aware of the danger signs. Mantel (1997) listed several factors that could point to an employee's potential for violence. These include:

- disaffection from the workplace resulting from real or perceived injustices;

- social isolation;

- poor self-esteem;

- fascination with weapons;

- difficulty with impulse and/or anger management;

- a history of verbal or physical threats and aggression towards others, including supervisors;

- an unstable family life;

- previous involvement in union-management disputes;

- a history of physical and/or emotional problems that have been unresponsive to treatment;

- regular complaints about working conditions and their job description;

- high stress levels at work;

- male between 30 and 40;

- dubious work history;

- history of drug and/or alcohol abuse; and/or

- has a diagnosable mental health problem (In Randall, 1997:53).

Geffner, Braverman, Galasso & Marsh (2004:83) suggest that "aggressive personalities" are identifiable through their "desire or motive to overcome opposition forcefully, to fight, to revenge an injury, to attack another with intent to injure or kill, and to oppose forcefully or punish another".

Other authors point out that frequent choice of aggression to deal with frustration, dislike of the subject of the aggression, the desire to inflict injury on another, and a lack of impulse control may all contribute to highly anti-social behavior in the workplace (O'Leary-Kelly, Griffin & Pritchard, 2004).

Ignoring workplace harassment can lead to serious and sometimes tragic escalation that would not otherwise occur. Consider the case of Theresa Vince, a 25 year employee of Sears Canada Inc. Theresa was described as "highly competent" and "the one who runs the store" by other employees (MacQuarrie, Welsh, Huntley, & Carr, 2004). She had an exemplary record and had enjoyed both her co-workers and work environment until a new manager arrived on the scene. Sixteen months prior to the tragic events that would lead to her death, she made a complaint concerning a "poisoned work environment" and "sexual harassment" by her new manager. Nothing was done. Over time, this confident, energetic woman exhibited difficulty sleeping, was unable to eat, and showed signs of depression. On June 2, 1996, as her early retirement date was approaching, her manager shot her to death and turned the gun on himself. What became clear in the coroner's inquest that followed was that many people were aware of what Theresa was being subjected to, but no one intervened on her behalf to stop the harassment.

Unfortunately there is a common "it can't happen here" attitude in many companies and organizations, and so preventative action is not taken. Often policies and procedures, educational workshops for managers and employees, and assistance to victims are remedies implemented after someone has been emotionally or physically injured or killed.

Tragedies like those of Theresa Vince can be avoided where managers act quickly to address the actions of those who subject others to psychological or other forms of harassment in the workplace. The best form of prevention is the establishment of a workplace culture and climate where anti-social and disruptive behaviors are not tolerated, and result in serious consequences for perpetrators.

REFERENCES

American Psychiatric Association. (2000). *Diagnostic and statistical manual of mental disorders (DSM-IV-TR)*. 4rth Ed. Washington, D.C.

Babiak, P. & Hare, R.D. (2006). *Snakes in suits: When psychopaths go to work*. N.Y.: HarperCollins

Cahn, D.D. & Abigail, R.A. (2006). *Managing conflict through communication*. Boston, MA.: Pearson Allyn and Bacon

Canada Safety Council. (2007). *Bullying in the workplace.* Retrieved June 5, 2007 from: www.safety-council.org/info/OSH/bullies.html

Canadian Alliance on Mental Illness. (2006). *Brief to the House of Commons Standing Committee on Finance: PreBudget Deliberations.* Retrieved June 15, 2007 from: http://www.cpa.ca/cpasite/ userfiles/Documents/advocacy/CAMHMI%20Brief%20to%20Fin ance%20Committee%202006%20Final.pdf

Crick, N. R., & Dodge, K. A. (1994). A Review and Reformulation of Social Information-Processing Mechanisms in Children's Social Adjustment." *Psychological Bulletin, 115*, 74–101.

Geffner, R. (Ed), Braverman, M, Galasso, J. Marsh, J. (2005). *Aggression in organizations: Violence, abuse and harassment at work and in schools.* Binghamton, NY: Haworth Maltreatment and Trauma Press.

Hare, R.D. & Babiak, P. (2006). *Snakes in suits.* N.Y.: HarperCollins.

James, L.R., McIntyre, M.D., Glisson, C.A., Green, P.D., Patton, T.W., LeBreton, J.M, Frost, B.C., Russell, S.M., Sablynski, C.J., Mitchell, T.R., & Williams, L.J. (2005). A conditional reasoning measure for aggression. *Organizational Research Methods,* (8)(1), pgs. 69-99 Thousand Oaks, CA: Sage Publications.

MacQuarrie, B., Welsh, S., Huntley, A., & Carr, J. (2004). *Workplace harassment and violence report.* London, Ontario: Centre for Research on Violence Against Women and Children. University of Western Ontario.

Namie, G. (November/December, 2003). Workplace bullying Escalated incivility. London, Ontario: *Ivey Business Journal Online.*

Namie, G., & Namie, R. (2003). *The bully at work.* Naperville, Ill: Sourcebooks, Inc.

National Institute for Occupational Safety and Health. (July 28, 2004). *Most workplace bullying is worker to worker early findings of NIOSH study suggest.* Centers for Disease Control and Prevention. Retrieved July 15, 2007 from: www.dcd.gov/niosh/updates/upd-07-28-04.html

O'Leary-Kelly, A., Griffin, R.W., & Pritchard, R.D. (2004) *The dark side of organizational behavior.* Mississauga, Ontario: John Wiley and Sons Canada Ltd.

Personnel Today. (September 20, 2005 & September 15, 2005). *Bullying beats a path to management's door.* Retrieved June 15, 2007 from: http://www.personneltoday.com/Articles/2005/09/15/31602/uk-managers-become-victims-in-fight-to-beat-the-bullies.html

Personnel Today. (November 7, 2006) *Bullies use covert tactics to antagonize colleagues.* Retrieved July 21, 2007 from: http://www.personneltoday.com/Articles/2006/11/07/38037/bullies-use-covert-tactics-to-antagonise-colleagues.html

Randall, P. (1997). *Adult bullying: Perpetrators and victims.* London and NY: Routledge.

Salin, D. (2003). *Way of explaining workplace bullying: A review of enabling, motivating and precipitating structures and processes in the work environment,* 56,1213-1232.

Simpson, J. W. (May 10, 2006) Psychopaths wear suits too. *Financial Post.* Retrieved July 20, 2007 from: http://working.canada.com/ottawa/sectors/story.html?s_id=PQPzd95UjpW%2FQG6Ko2vqJd9NCzYTKUKdUI4JWPckKm46oftAWaxEtg%3D%3D

Spector, P.E. & Fox, S. (2005). *Stressor-emotion model.* In S. Fox and P.E. Spector (Eds) *Counterproductive work behavior: Investigations of actors and targets.* Washington, DC: American Psychological Association.

Talbot, C. (2004). *Psychological harassment up this year in Canadian business.* Retrieved January 9, 2007 from: http://hrpao.org/HRPAO/knowledgeCentre/newsc...

U.K. National Bullying Advice Line. (2006) *History and statistics.* Retrieved January 12, 2007 from: bullyonline.org/workbully/ worbal.htm

CHAPTER THREE

Who are the most likely targets?

When someone is targeted for bullying, the first question they often ask is "why me"? Whether or not bullies are able to target individuals in organizations often has more to do with the organizational culture than with a target's characteristics. Role ambiguity or role conflict, and weak or inadequate organizational leadership, along with a lack of control and a generally negative work environment can lay the groundwork for bullies to begin jockeying for position (Beswick, Gore & Palferman, 2006).

Unfortunately in some organizations the immediate question that is asked when someone reports being mobbed or bullied is "what did they do to deserve it?" Many still believe the myth that it is the underperformers in an organization who are subject to bullying behavior by others.

This is not the case according to the literature, and this "blame the victim" approach is also not helpful, indicates a lack of knowledge about this subject, and may, in fact, make the problem worse. Workplace bullies thrive in workplaces where targets are not believed or are blamed.

Adams (October 11, 2006) says "... contrary to common perception, targets of workplace bullies aren't the underachievers, the slackers and the deadwood. Often they're very capable and productive employees whose competence threatens the bully".

The consensus in the literature is that anyone can be bullied or mobbed in the workplace.

"Individuals can be victimized no matter who they are, how old, devoted, loyal, creative, experienced, organized, responsible, how much initiative they demonstrate, or how much a team player they are" (Davenport, Schwartz & Elliott, 2002:71). Individuals with a "high degree of loyalty towards their organizations... [who are] highly identified with their work", are more likely to be mobbed, as are "highly creative individuals [because] they promote new ideas which may challenge others".

If you are "nice", not only are you likely to be bullied, but you are also not likely to be promoted (Lehoczky, 2004). The Boston Globe reports "After surveying white-collar workers in Britain, University of Sheffield researcher Nikos Bozionelos found that those with the most agreeable personalities were less likely to be promoted. In fact, Bozionelos found that being conscientious and pleasant might do your career more harm than good".

"Victims [of workplace bullying] tend to be highly skilled at their jobs and very self directed". According to Namie, quoted in the Boston Globe article, "it's no wonder, then, that bullying incidents are frequently reported by members of ''helper'' professions such as nursing, teaching and counseling.".

The Canadian Safety Council (2007) suggests that "the target chosen by an adult bully will very often be a capable, dedicated staff member, well liked by co-workers. Bullies are most likely to pick on people with an ability to cooperate and a non-confrontative interpersonal style. The bully considers their capability a threat, and determines to cut them down".

Targets are often "highly conscientious, more traditional, and may be more rigid and moralistic" thereby causing potential perpetrators anxiety (Coyne, Seigne, & Randall, 2000).

Zapf & Einarsen (2003) explain that targets who may clash with established group norms are more open to hostility and attack because of their difference, or perceived disengagement from the group. This perceived disengagement frustrates colleagues and may lead to retaliation.

The phenomenon of individuals being targeted for their refusal to participate in established group norms – even unethical ones, also appeared in interviews conducted for this book. Those who would not go along with unethical, unprofessional, or substandard work or conduct were generally targeted by others who felt threatened by them.

Mobbing occurred when "groupthink" took over, and the individual who refused to compromise her or his own professional standards or personal values was targeted for attack by others who had been only too willing to compromise theirs.

The "ratebuster, whistleblower, champion of the underdog, the person who asks too many questions" also tends to be a target (Davenport, Schwartz, & Elliott, 2002:72).

Others may be vulnerable because of their life circumstances – deaths of loved ones, illness, concerns about children, parents, or financial difficulties (Davenport, Schwartz & Elliott, 2002:73). Workplace bullies, sensing weakness, may target them.

This view is parallel to recent research done on sexual harassment in the workplace. Dr. Jennifer Berdahl, a business professor at the Rotman School of Management, University of Toronto has said that even sexual harassment appears to be motivated more by hostility toward "uppity women" who do not conform to "gender ideals" than by desire or anything else. She also discusses how non-sexual harassment has become more predominant. "…professional women compared to men report significantly more incivility and aggression – behaviors that alienate the victim, rather than approaching them sexually" (Berdahl & Cortina, 2007 In press).

Workplace bullies may also be triggered by their victims' competence or whistleblowing activities. Namie and Namie (2003:5) say, "research and anecdotal evidence show that it is the emotionally unintelligent perpetrators who escalate their tyrannical misconduct when they feel threatened by, and react in response to targets' asserted independence, technical and social skills, or ethical whistle blowing". They suggest that bright, creative, and self-assured people committed to ethical work habits pose the greatest threat to workplace bullies, and may therefore be targeted out of fear of exposure, or envy. It is "bullied targets – often the most talented employees, [who] are driven from the workplace".

> *Cynthia, a bright young woman with exceptional clinical and community development skills, took over as a manager of an agency providing services to children. Eager to do a good job, she began to actively engage the community in her work, establishing excellent relationships with community members. Unbeknownst to her, others in the organization had applied for her position but did not get it, and were now having to report to her.*

The corporate office was ostensibly supportive, even counseling her in how to fire staff members who were incompetent or insubordinate. Little did she know that a person or persons in the corporate office would later collude with these same staff to drive her out as they had done with several others before her. She was even warned by several of these former employees about how her treatment would follow a "recipe" and she was shocked when it did.

The thing that is sometimes most shocking about bullying behavior is that it follows such a predictable pattern. It is almost possible to anticipate the bully's next move, which is why most targets are constantly on the lookout for particular kinds of behavior, and often see the patterns in the behavior long before others notice them. Of course, this, in some ways, contributes to targets being seen as "paranoid" by others who have failed to notice the bully's machinations, and their effects.

First she was undermined as corporate officers colluded with her staff behind her back. She was shown disrespect at meetings, and comments were made to her of a personal rather than professional nature by corporate staff. She was accused of having a conflict of interest because of a private practice that she was engaged in when she had been careful to ensure that this was not the case. She was subjected to constant attacks and challenges to her authority. She was told complaints were made against her, but never told what the exact nature of the complaints were or who had made them. This denial of administrative fairness continued for months. Finally, after all else failed, a staff member who Cynthia later learned had been colluding with someone in the corporate office, accused her of sexual harassment – an allegation that was not true.

Where targets refuse to succumb to the bullying tactics, valiantly attempting to hold onto their jobs, positions, or reputations, bullying will often escalate to a more serious level. The problem with serious allegations, even if they are untrue, is that they are very difficult to refute. It is much harder to prove one's innocence than it is to accuse someone. Attempting to fight even serious allegations is often costly on a personal and financial level. And if a bully is not particularly well off, it may not even be worth the target attempting to sue them. Some targets have now opted to sue their employers for failing to ensure a safe workplace. This will be discussed in more detail in a later chapter.

Unable to deal with the stress of the constant harassment, Cynthia negotiated her way out of the organization. Later, one of the individuals at the corporate office who had colluded against her with her own staff, and who was envious because she had a position he wanted, was given her job. He wanted to relocate to the geographical area that she was working in, and arranged a campaign of harassment, colluding with others inside the organization to orchestrate his successfully bumping her out of her position so that he could take it.

In this case the bully had a specific goal in mind – usurping Cynthia's position. As previously mentioned, attempting to obtain a personal benefit is often enough cause for a bully to personally attack or undermine someone.

During the entire six months that she was subjected to constant harassment, no one inside the organization came to her aid. The only people who supported her were her predecessors, all of whom had been subjected to the exact same treatment by the corporate office.

The impact on Cynthia was enormous. Even though this was a well rehearsed campaign of constant harassment that was a repeat of harassment directed at her predecessors, Cynthia was left feeling she could not defend herself, and feeling embarrassed at, and hurt by the serious, albeit false allegation of sexual harassment made against her.

She had always had a good reputation and was deeply concerned that irrespective of her innocence of the charge, that it could damage her good name and interfere with her future professional endeavors. Even though she had done nothing wrong, she was left with the cloud of suspicion forever hanging over her head.

Worse than that was the self doubt that she endured. The constant harassment had undermined her sense of self. Fencing with shadowy accusations and accusers for months, she was emotionally depleted and physically exhausted. She had lost her confidence as a manager, was always bracing herself in case of further victimization, had trouble eating and sleeping, and was unable to perform work that she had always done with ease.

The legacy of her mistreatment remains with her over a decade after it occurred, and in spite of her having been able to go on into very high profile and important positions, where her skills were highly valued by a great many people, she feels forever changed by the harassment she endured.

According to Barash (2006), a professor of gender studies at Marymount Manhattan College, highly accomplished women are more likely to be the targets of woman on woman aggression as well. "Envy, competition, and jealousy underlie the sometimes deceitful and treacherous way that some women deal with others. This is the often unspoken dark side of female relationships, and it can result in the loss of many organizations' brightest stars".

Dedication, Values, and Ethics As Red Flags?

Davenport, Schwartz & Elliot (2002:70) found that people who were mobbed were more likely to be exceptional in some way – dedicated, accomplished, competent, and emotionally intelligent. Many were "nice" people. Namie & Namie (2003:40) report that "bullies eat nice people alive", and welcome the opportunity to work with a bunch of "cooperators" who they can boss around and terrorize with sadistic glee. The main reason that nice people are targeted according to the authors is that they are envied for their likeability, or their tendency to be self-effacing.

Dr. Kenneth Westhues (2002), in writing about academia, stated that professors who were not "go with the flow" sort of people, and who could be described as "principled" were more likely to be mobbed. Having ethics appears to be a major risk factor for being bullied in organizations. This also appears to be particularly true in settings like nursing, social work, law enforcement, and other areas where the "we feeling" can be disrupted when a professional takes their role and responsibilities seriously and reports a co-worker for unprofessional or unethical conduct. Namie & Name (2003:42) point out that those who are targeted often have "impractical expectations" about how organizations, employees and employers should treat each other.

Basic expectations concerning integrity in how people carry out their jobs will often set individuals up for bullying. The goal of the bully who targets someone because of their integrity or ethics is to silence them. The fear is that if these individuals are not "taken out" the bully's own unethical conduct with be exposed, and their career could be hurt. Often these bullies have more than enough supporters in the workplace – other individuals who also fear that the target will tell the truth about their own lack of professionalism or integrity. In this scenario the target is seen as a threat, and the favorite battle tactic is character assassination. The one thing targets hold dear, something that often took them a lifetime to build – their character and/or reputation, is under attack, and the results can be devastating.

The High Achiever's Dilemma

This presents a difficult dilemma for the high achievers, those with personal integrity, and "nice people" who populate our workplaces, since their very competence and "niceness" may place them right in an envious or resentful bully's sights.

Clearly most would not choose to have to be less competent or nice simply to avoid attack, however, there may be something to be said for developing a "work persona" – the mask many have learned to wear, especially in toxic work environments. By being civil but otherwise revealing little personal or professional information, some have managed to stay out of a bully's way.

But is this enough? Likely not. Since aside from being more conscientious or having good values, there is little else to distinguish a target from those not targeted by aggressive workplace bullies (Zapf & Einarsen, 2005), there is likely nothing a bullied employee can do to escape once they are targeted, except leave. Fighting back may help in some circumstances, provided that the bully does not thrive on the conflict, in which case it may exacerbate things.

Signal For a Life Change?

Could there be a hidden, more mysterious process at work when someone finds her of himself bullied by another in the workplace? Interview information showing that for many, there is simply no escape, also turned up another possibility. Interestingly, some respondents reported that being bullied signaled the need for a life change. Some reported looking back on the incident, and realizing that it was the beginning of a necessary and positive change in their lives. Had the bullying never happened, they may never have changed course. For some, as difficult and hurtful as the experience was, it brought about what they later saw as needed change in themselves and in their life circumstances.

Personal Histories of Early Trauma?

Bullies, being typical predators, see self-denigrating statements as "tell tale signs of a deeper insecurity" that may have occurred much earlier in a target's life. This makes them prime candidates for attack, since the seeds of self-doubt have already been planted by a predecessor.

This is consistent with the literature on child abuse that suggests that individuals who were traumatized earlier in their lives may be traumatized again later in life (Anderson, 2002). The constant replay of perceived persecution, futile attempts to escape, and revictimization can wear some targets down to the point where they become depressed and contemplate suicide.

This is one of the things that makes psychological harassment so dangerous. No one knows what another person's personal history has been. When predators attack, even they may be unaware of the degree to which they set off an internal chain reaction in their targets by triggering original feelings of unworthiness or unbearable pain. It is these internal reactions that can lead to sometimes devastating consequences.

Personal Vulnerability Due To Life Circumstances?

Bullies also often choose their targets during a time when the target is vulnerable because of personal grief and loss, trauma, health issues, or challenges that are occurring in their personal lives. Most bullies will leave strong and competent people alone while they are at full strength, usually resorting only to cowardly passive aggressive actions. However, once they sense vulnerability, they will strike with a vengeance against a weakened unwitting target. Of course it is at times like these that their attacks are also likely to do the most harm.

Almost every person interviewed for this book indicated that they had been attacked at a time in their lives when they were psychologically weakened because of a personal loss of some kind. Some had recently broken up long term relationships, others had suffered an illness, others had suffered deaths in their family. It would appear that workplace bullies exhibit a kind of archetypal predatory behavior. They attack their targets when they perceive them to be in a weakened state and less likely to fight back or get away.

This may also explain why competent individuals with passive personalities also find themselves victimized repeatedly. Smart predators do not attack individuals who they perceive as strong, healthy, and more than ready to take them on. Sometimes they wait to gain their advantage. True workplace warriors, they use proven tactics by waiting to strike when the perceived "enemy" is least able to defend him or herself.

Namie & Namie (2003:30) report that paradoxically some workplace predators may "also target strong people for assault" because of their refusal to be "subservient" or "go along with being controlled". The attacks often take the form of undermining behavior, where there are attempts made to set the target up to fail in some way. The favorite battle tactics used in these scenarios are sabotage and disinformation campaigns. Fearing a counterattack by a more powerful adversary, they resort to these kinds of passive-aggressive behaviors to attempt to gain an advantage.

The Organizational Bellwether

It is often the "bellwether" in an organization – the individual who has always been the organization's best performer who first shows signs that an increasingly toxic environment may be developing because of psychological warfare. If these individuals begin to show serious morale problems, or a loss of commitment to the organization, senior managers should consider assertively determining the cause. Bellwethers are the best determinants of culture and climate in organizations. Often likeable and tuned in to others in the workplace, they tend to be the ones to whom others turn when things are going wrong. Wise managers listen to them if they begin to sound the alarm. Inadequate or incompetent mangers ignore them at their own peril.

Unfortunately even the most capable employees hesitate to speak up about their mistreatment. Namie (2003:3) has reported that targets of workplace bullying endure their pain, on average, for 22 months". Unwilling to react to aggression with aggression, many targets choose to keep their torment hidden until they can no longer bear it.

Why Don't You Speak Up For Yourself?

Even though most targets are bright, capable people, the wearing effect of constant bullying can undermine even their self-confidence. When people ask why targets don't speak up for themselves, they are asking from the privileged position of someone who has never been targeted.

Targets do not speak up because the bully has often undermined and isolated them for some time, and speaking up would have little or no effect. Most targets are smart enough to know that.

Targets also know that many bosses could not care less, and do not want to be bothered with "interpersonal issues". Most are ignorant of the extremely damaging impact of bullying in their workplaces until it arrives at their own front doors. Targets know that trying to "educate" an ignorant boss (who may even be the harasser) is a waste of time.

Self doubt has also often crept into the equation. Constant emotional attack can do that to even the most self assured target. No one is able to withstand constant attacks on one's credibility, professionalism, abilities, or reputation over a lengthy period of time.

Some bullies love a good fight, and targets know that getting into confrontations with them would only add to the bully's enjoyment and escalate the situation even further. In some cases, one of the last bits of control left to them is to not give the bully the satisfaction of having engaged them in a confrontation. Besides, most competent and caring "targets" have better things to do than to scrap with a bully who enjoys nothing more than creating conflict.

Payback Time?

One of the dangers mentioned consistently in the literature is the danger that at some point a line will have been crossed, and even the most competent, reasonable, and non-violent targets may finally strike back. According to Keashly & Harvey (2005) "Prolonged exposure to abuse can result in the target behaving in a hostile and aggressive manner, both actively (eg verbal outbursts, physical assault), and passively (withholding organizational citizenship behaviors, silent treatment). Such responses may fuel escalatory spirals that may lead to physical violence (Glomb, 2002), or the spreading of hostility to initially uninvolved others (Anderson and Pearson, 1999)".

Unfortunately, when a target finally "loses it" and strikes back, it is they who are likely to face the consequences, not the bully. Bullies lie and embellish situations, and may use the target's loss of composure as an excuse to file a complaint or take other action, portraying themselves as the victims.

Sadly, too often those in the position to address this insidious problem are unaware that victims can, at times, look like victimizers. Driven to distraction by constant onslaughts, targets can themselves become irritable and snap at others. Embarrassed by what is happening to them, they may choose to keep the source of their torment quiet. When they finally do speak up, as Namie & Namie (2003:46) have said, they may "appear angry to co-workers and management ..... pent up resentment toward the bully comes spewing out angrily and unfiltered". Unsure of how to respond to this level of anger, and subject to projective identification, where they may experience the target's anger as their own, bosses may become annoyed with the target. This dynamic can easily lead to the revictimization of the target.

Any manager seeking to address the issue of workplace bullying must keep foremost in her or his mind, the preponderance of evidence. Has the target always been a good employee? Have they only recently appeared distant, uncommunicative, and disengaged? Has the alleged harasser had other problems, or is he or she recently arrived in the workplace with little or no previous track record? By "drilling down" to the bare facts, managers can often easily determine who has been victimized, even in a "she said, she said" scenario.

REFERENCES

Adams, S. (October 11, 2006). Workplace bullying hitting bottom lines. *Business Edge*. . 6(23). Retrieved February 12, 2007 from: http://www.businessedge.ca/article.cfm/newsID/13969.cfm

Anderson, C. (2002). Workplace violence: What factors may be putting you at risk? *AWHONN Lifelines*, 6(30), 212-214.

Anderson, L.M & Pearson, C.M. (1999). Tit for tat? The spiraling effect of incivility in the workplace. *Academy of Management Review*, 24, 452-471.

Barash, S.S. (2006). *Tripping the prom queen: the truth about women and rivalry*. St. Martin's Press.

Berdahl, J.L & Cortina, L.M. (2007 In Press). *Sexual harassment in organizations: A decade of research in review*. In C. Cooper and J. Barling (Eds) *Handbook of Organizational Behavior*. Thousand Oaks, CA: Sage.

Berhdahl, J.L. (2007). *Gender and social undermining in the workplace*. Paper presented at the 22nd annual meeting of the Society of Industrial and Organizational Psychology, 2007.

Beswick, J., Gore, J., & Palferman, D. (2006). *Health and safety laboratory – Bullying at work: A review of the literature*. Science Group: Human Factors.

Canada Safety Council. (2007). *Bullying in the workplace*. Retrieved February, 21, 2007 from: http://www.safety-council.org/info/OSH/bullies.html

Coyne, I, Seigne, E., Randall, P. (2000). Predicting workplace victim status from personality. *European Journal of Work and Organizationa. Psychology*. 9(3). Pgs. 335 – 349.

Davenport, N., Schwartz, R.D., Elliott, G.P. (2002). *Mobbing emotional abuse in the American workplace*. Ames, Iowa: Civil Society Publishing

Glomb, T.M. (2002). Workplace aggression: Informing conceptua. models with data from specific encounters. *Journal of Occupationa. Health Psychology*, 7, 20-36.

Keashly, L, & Harvey, S. (2005). *Workplace emotional abuse.* Retrieved March 18, 2007 from: *http://www.sagepub.com/upm-data/8745_ KellowayCh6.pdf*

Lehoczky, E. (November 21, 2004). The bully principle: Nice workers more likely to get pushed around, less likely to be promoted. *The Boston Globe.*

Namie, G. (2003) Workplace bullying: Escalated incivility? *Ivey Business Journal Online.* Richard Ivey School of Business. University of Western Ontario.

Namie, G, Namie, R. (2003). *The bully at work.* Naperville, Illinois: Sourcebooks Inc.

Salin, D. (2003). *Workplace bullying among business professionals: Prevalence and organizational antecedents and gender differences.* Helsinki, Finland: Swedish School of Economics and Business Management.

Westhues, K. (1998). *Eliminating professors: A guide to the dismissal process.* Queenston, Canada: Kempner Collegium Publications.

Westhues, K. (2002). *Human sacrifice in universities: Toronto versus Richardson.* Lewiston, N.Y.: Kempner Collegium Publications.

Westhues, K. (2004). *Workplace mobbing in academe: Reports from twenty universities. Lewiston,* NY: Edwin Mellen Press.

Zapf, D. & Einarsen, S. (2003). *Individual antecedents of bullying: Victims and perpetrators.* In Einarsen, S, Hoel, H, Zapf, D. and Cooper, C. (Eds). *Bullying and emotional abuse in the workplace: International perspectives in research and practice.* London: Taylor & Francis.

CHAPTER FOUR

The High Cost of Whistleblowing

Matthiesen (2004) has defined whistleblowing as "the act that takes place when an employee is witnessing wrongdoing in the workplace (e.g. unethical conduct, corruption, violence, bullying against others, criminal acts) from a fellow employee or a superior (or a group of employees or superiors), and he or she then tries to stop the wrongdoing by informing a leader or someone who is in the position to stop it. This telling about the wrongdoing may be done internally or externally."

Matthiesen explains the difference between "informing" and "whistleblowing" as the whistleblower "not taking action with the intent to promote their own career ambitions". Informers attempt to "get even" with others in their workplaces, while whistleblowers often act to attempt to promote quality service, public safety, or prevent injury, the loss of lives, or to address human rights violations.

Matthiesen also says that whistleblowing is often tied to "important ethical or societal issues", and that the whistleblower does not "have the conscience to just keep quiet".

This means that whistleblowers are a special breed. Raised with strong values and imbued with personal integrity, often through the influence of an important early caregiver, they consider the truth to be worth defending – often at any price. They are the Joan of Arcs of the workplace, people who risk censure, persecution, and sometimes personal harm, to remain true to an ideal.

Those who are not whistleblowers find it difficult to understand what motivates people who appear to take enormous personal risks for little or no personal gain. Others are suspicious of them. They consider them to be driven by some internal demons which they do not understand. Most scratch their heads and ask themselves "what is wrong with these people?" Unable to understand why whistleblowers do not just go with the flow, or recognize that some things are not worth fighting for, or that practicalities demand that they acquiesce, those who do not whistleblow find their own values and personal integrity challenged by those who do. And therein lies the problem.

Whistleblowers are often targets of envy, feelings of shame, and anger by those who do not live by their own principles. Those most likely to sell out for the sake of a promotion, or to ingratiate themselves to someone in a position of authority, are also most likely to despise the whistleblowers in their midst and target them in an effort to silence them or drive them out of the workplace.

Whistleblowers are constant reminders of what decent people ought to be doing, but often do not do. They are compelled to tell the truth, to expose wrongs, to correct injustices. Their refusal to let things go, and to persist in advancing their causes, makes them targets for those who do not wish to be reminded of their responsibilities, their professional ethics, or their need to stand by their own values.

We like to celebrate whistleblowers in films like Norma Rae, but when it comes to the Norma Raes in our own organizations, we tend to see them simply as irritants – people who we wish would just go away. They are the ones who make our lives more complicated. We grate at their constant insistence that they are right and we are wrong. We consider them to be insufferable and sanctimonious.

Those of us who prefer a kinder interpretation simply see them as "quaint", people who just don't get it that they need to be a bit more pragmatic and not fight every battle. Their actions and thought processes are considered to be naïve, lacking in understanding of the forces that drive a workplace – power and influence, profit and loss, career advancement and self interest.

To others, whistleblowers seem to come from another planet. It is hard to even understand what they are talking about. Those who come from families where making money and acquiring material goods are the ultimate accomplishment, simply do not understand when whistleblowers start talking about doing what is right, or serving a higher purpose, or righting a wrong.

To workplace bullies, whistleblowers are grist for the mill. Their naïve adherence to principles readies them to be portrayed as objects of ridicule, and targets for character assassination. Because bullies do not play by the same rules as whistleblowers, they find it easy to undermine them by spreading lies and disinformation.

Whistleblowers, being honest themselves, often make the assumption that others will deal with them honestly. This sets the stage for bullies to behave duplicitously, gaining a whistleblower's trust, then destroying them through betrayal.

In some cases, whistleblower's lives have been threatened by bullies with enormous power, influence and wealth. Such was the case with Melanie.

Melanie had been a top notch emergency room nurse, and had worked in intensive care and trauma units. Her experience was extensive.

According to her, after the tragic death of her husband, Melanie moved across the country with her children, and went to work in a nursing home. When she discovered that the nursing home was stockpiling narcotic medications with little or no controls, she blew the whistle to the Health Ministry. When she discovered fraudulent practices she blew the whistle to everyone, including elected officials and the Labour Board. No one listened to her. When the nursing home chain went bankrupt, she confronted the owners about the fraudulent practices at a creditors' meeting. After that, her life became a living hell.

She was followed and warned by other employees that her house would be burned down. She thought they were "just talking". She was wrong. Weeks later her home was burned to the ground. Smoke detectors went off as flames came out of the laundry chute. She had noticed an unfamiliar blue van parked outside of her house some time before it started burning. A box containing clothes with tissue paper that was found at the bottom of the laundry chute was given to the fire department and promptly disappeared. The Fire Marshall's office was useless. His sister worked in a long term care facility.

In spite of having been interviewed on several occasions by a female police officer, no records of the interviews were located at the local police detachment.

An insurance investigator's report said that the official cause of the blaze was undetermined.

A local lawyer who offered to assist her turned out to be connected to the owners of the nursing home.

She lost her job, and she lost her life. Luckily she and her children escaped unharmed, but she had been subjected to intruders, phone calls, rumor mongering, and threats of physical injury

While still working, she became a target of mobbing, and was screamed and yelled at by her superiors in front of her patients.

She suffered significant emotional distress and still fears for her life and the lives of her children. She received counseling for traumatic stress. Her attempts to stand by her professional standards and principles almost cost her her life.

Unfortunately Melanie's story is not an isolated incident, although it is an extreme example of how far bullies will go to silence someone. Everywhere whistleblowers try to do the right thing, they are castigated, harassed, and threatened with their jobs, well being, or their lives. There are very few workplaces that value their whistleblowers or see them as important early warning systems.

Consider the case of Dan. Dan was employed by the government as a policy analyst. Bright, committed, and with a great deal of personal integrity, Dan's problems started when his dad was treated badly by the health care system. Devastated by his father's ordeal, and wishing to ensure that no one else would have to go through similar circumstances, Dan launched a private foundation to help individuals and families navigate their way through the system.

He was called on the carpet by his boss and told that the foundation he had organized was a conflict of interest with his work. Apparently the government was not supposed to be in the business of helping people to navigate the services it funded.

Dan disagreed, stating that his work with the foundation was not a conflict of interest since other civil servants also did volunteer work with non-profit organizations.

He was subjected to constant pressure about his involvement with the organization, in spite of his attempts to appease his employers. He was told to either choose the organization or his job. Feeling worn down emotionally and physically, and also involved in his father's continuing medical malpractice suit, he withdrew from the non-profit organization. He described himself as feeling "scared, tired, and intimidated".

He also began to experience detrimental emotional effects because of his treatment and was forced to take a medical leave of absence for two years. He could not focus, he had insomnia, and suffered from depression for which he was treated with anti-depressants.

All of these effects have been described again and again by those who have had to endure bullying in the workplace. Anxiety and depression are very common features of target's personalities. Sadly, the fact of their having developed a mental illness because of what amounts to emotional torture, can result in them being fired for their inability to do their job. In a horribly ironic twist, the bully is then left free to target someone else.

A short time after his leave began, an article that he had been interviewed for at a much earlier date appeared in a prominent magazine. His employer responded to this with a letter of insubordination being placed in his file.

He was asked to attend a mediation session with his employer where he was told by the mediator that there was a conflict of interest, and he was offered a "buyout" to leave his position. He was told that if he returned to work he could not contribute even his own money to his foundation, or attend fundraisers, and he would be required to provide proof that he had no further involvement with the foundation. Finally exhausted, he agreed to the buyout and a gag order, but never actually signed the contract.

When he went into his office to clean out his desk, he found nothing there. He was told by a co-worker that the boss had ordered his office cleaned out. Angry and distraught that his personal belongings had been removed to an unknown location, he "lost it" and began to shout. He said afterwards that he realized he did himself no favors by finally losing his temper.

This is another common outcome of bullying. The target ends up finally having a "meltdown" when he or she can endure no more. This is then often seen as justification for the mistreatment she or he has received. History is rewritten to suggest that it was this kind of "emotional" behavior that was problematic from the start.

Dan's own lawyer even told him that he did not want to go too hard at the government because he "had to work with them". His own union accused him of being "unreasonable". He had no allies at all at work, only his family members, who knew him best.

Off work, and with his funds running out, he accepted a transfer to another government Ministry where he was not given much to do. He was also told by his superior there that she "hoped he would not embarrass the government". Gossip about him had apparently followed him to his new place of employment.

Angered that he was being denied the right of every other government employee to do volunteer work with non-profit organizations, he rejoined his foundation. He promptly received a letter from his employer suspending him with pay because of his involvement. He was also invited to attend a meeting with his previous boss to explain his involvement in the foundation. His previous employer was "being really nice" according to Dan, so he went with a union rep. He ended up being fired with cause.

Very upset he contacted the press and several stories ran in major papers and on television. He launched a formal grievance concerning his firing, and wrote a twenty five page chronology of his treatment that was sent to the Minister.

The arbitrator's report, which according to Dan, included errors of omission of key evidence, and which dismissed a previously perfect HR record, and was "selective and biased", found against him. During the same period, his mother broke her hip.

Often there is absolutely no recourse for those who attempt to fight back against workplace bullying. Very few employers understand the problem, much less have policies and procedures to address it. Dan's workplace was a perfect example of this. With nothing to go on in the way of policies and procedures concerning psychological harassment, Dan was left with little choice but to use the existing mechanisms – all of which proved inadequate under the circumstances.

Depressed and out of money, he says that his whole life has changed, and he has to start all over again. Fortunately he has the support of his family, but the aftermath of his ordeal will likely remain with him for a lifetime.

Bullies have trouble understanding the people who live by their convictions. Those who lack conscience or empathy are particularly unable to find any common ground with those whose lives are dominated by care and concern for others, and driven by conscience. In bullies' eyes they simply make great targets, easy prey. Their honesty and desire to make the world a better place makes them vulnerable to those whose only goal is their own self-aggrandizement, advancement, or personal power.

Some cases of whistleblowing have made it into the public domain. In every case, the results of whistleblowing activity show an alarming parallel – every whistleblower was harassed by those in authority in some way.

According to a CBC report "In 1998 two bureaucrats at the Foreign Affairs Department accused then-minister Lloyd Axworthy and several of the highest-ranking bureaucrats in his department of wasting over $2 billion on Canadian ambassadors' living quarters and operations between 1986 and 1998." John Guenette and Joanna Gualtieri noted the waste in several countries and red flagged the problem, but they said the bureau "seemed not to care" and that after they raised their concerns "their bosses harassed them for raising [them]". The result was "dead end jobs" and both ended up on stress leave.

There was a similar outcome for Shiv Chopra, Margaret Haydon and Gerard Lambert, scientists with the Federal government who "spoke out publicly about the [Federal] department's approval process and what they call the undue influence of the pharmaceutical industry" (Eggerston, August 31, 2004). All three were fired while they were on stress leave. The Federal Department predictably denied that it was because of their whistleblowing activities even though they had previously told a committee reviewing the approval of bovine growth hormone that they feared reprisals - a familiar refrain.

Whistleblowers are all too familiar with the machinations of bullies who try to cover their actions with fabrications and disinformation.

> Jane calls it a "decimating experience – life altering". An exceptional student who graduated with a degree in Psychology at 19, and was later called to the bar but did not end up going into practice, she worked for the Federal government. Deferential and respectful by nature and diligent in her work, she said that she was "blown away by bureaucratic ineptitude and lack of attention [to important issues]}". Dismayed at the lack of response to serious concerns she was raising about how public funding was being spent, she continued to attempt to be conciliatory in her approach, but worked hard and tried to do a good job.

> Jane represents the feelings of so many other whistleblowers, "when you shut up and keep your job, you pay a price and deviate from your own moral code". She felt she had a right to say something when policies were not respected and money obtained from the public purse was wasted.

> In the beginning she honestly believed that if she only worked hard she would earn her supervisors' respect. She was wrong. As she put it, "they only hit you with a bigger hammer because you're threatening to the status quo".

So often even very intelligent whistleblowers display a kind of naivete – a belief that there is justice for those who work hard and are conscientious. Unfortunately in many modern workplaces no good deed goes unpunished, especially where hard work and competence are seen as threats to others who would prefer not to have to work too hard in order to obtain professional rewards that they believe are due them without having to produce.

Jane's tendency to write comprehensive memos about her concerns made her superiors nervous. They retaliated with a campaign of what she describes as "psychological terror". She was mocked, treated in a dismissive way in everyday interactions, her reality was constantly questioned, and everything she said was challenged – her "values, morality, even her understanding of words". She was told to take a writing course because her memos were "too thorough". Her boss tapped his pen on the table every time she spoke. Her promised reclassification did not come through. She was removed from a project she had worked on for over a year because she would not break the rules to "move the project along". She was constantly asked if she liked working there, and told that they could find her another job, and her boss wrote denigrating memos about her to his superiors.

The end result for her was that she became so consumed with self doubt, that if she wrote two sentences in a memo, she had to call her professor father first to make sure that what she wrote made sense.

Self doubt is one of the first things to surface for targets. Because they are often highly competent and conscientious, their first act is to examine themselves to see if there is something that they have done wrong, some mistake that they need to correct. It is this self doubt created by those seeking to undermine their confidence and self worth in order to damage them sufficiently to drive them out that is often the precursor for depression, anxiety, and other mental health effects. Their usual tendency to be reflective or to attempt to see others' perspectives is what actually works against them in this kind of situation.

Finally after a two hour meeting where she was given no warning of what was to take place, and not given any information about the allegations against her so that she could defend herself, she was deployed to a non-existent position. Her bosses announced to her co-workers that she was no longer in the job, removed her name plate, and put someone else into her position. Unable to cope any longer, she left in tears.

There was no process to fight back with, and she found herself in legal limbo. Her union would not help her, and her complaint under the Canada Labour Code Health and Safety legislation went nowhere. She lost at adjudication. Furthermore, in November of 2003, the Public Service Modernization Act removed the right for Federal employees in Canada to sue their employer. In spite of a Whistleblower Bill having been introduced, it does not restore employees' rights to sue. Instead complaints are referred to an administrative board.

Jane is sure that she was the subject of "behind the scenes maneuvering" against which she was unable to defend herself. In the end, only one other co-worker, with whom she had a personal relationship, even came to her aid. The impact on her family life has been devastating. Her husband does not work anymore and is as depressed and destroyed by what occurred as she is. Attempting to take her issue to court has only entrapped her further because as she describes it, she remains locked in a "continuous psychologically damaging situation". And lawsuits can go on for years.

Many whistleblowers who are badly treated by their organizations also describe a corporate culture that is crass, hard nosed, unwelcoming and generally disrespectful of employees. In Jane's case, swearing was rampant. Managers used phrases like "tell him to f…. himself". Divide and conquer games were played, and employees who did not fall in line were subject to smear campaigns. People and careers were damaged, and no one was held to account. The workplace was like a toxic palace of potential attacks. Even the most accomplished individual cannot expect to swim with corporate sharks who engage in these kinds of tactics, and actually survive.

Sarah's story illustrates so well why whistleblowers are often hated by co-workers and supervisors and subjected to campaigns of harassment that can drive them to drink. Those who are unwilling to sacrifice their professional competence and look the other way when others do, can find themselves at the receiving end of workplace attacks.

Sarah liked her job with older adults in the nursing home in which she worked. She cared about them and wanted them to be comfortable and feel cared for in their final years. She spent time upgrading her skills by going back to college, and wanted very much to put them to good use. Sadly, she was not the norm, and this is what made her a target.

When residents were burned by staff who put heat packs on them and then failed to supervise them, she initially covered for the home with the families who filed complaints. Riddled with guilt, and unlike others who were just there to "collect their pay cheques", Sarah decided that she had to take things up with her supervisor. The trouble was that afterwards her supervisor pretended they had never had any conversation about the heat pack problem, when in fact they had had several.

This is also a common problem. Where a target fails to document in writing having made a complaint, it is her word against a supervisor's or co-worker's.

Parallel to what happened to other whistleblowers, she was asked "if you're unhappy here why don't you leave?" This is often the first warning sign that a campaign of harassment is about to begin. It is a veritable warning shot across the bow of the whistleblower.

What followed was that things she said in meetings never made the minutes. Important things, like whether or not people washed their hands before providing care to someone else – a basic infection control procedure, were never included in written documentation when she raised them. When she reported serious breaches in the way that care was delivered, her reports were not followed up, and the excuses were rampant from her superiors – "if I come down on her I have to come down on everyone".

When she raised serious concerns about residents being given heat packs without any range of motion taking place as was required, she initially received no response from the home administrator. Not long after the administrator called her at home to remind her that "you are doing my job again".

It would be such a simple matter for supervisors to address concerns like these. Unfortunately too many begin to see whistleblowers' actions as an attempt at control rather than an attempt to set things right. So many workplace difficulties could be avoided if only supervisors would pay attention to these whistleblowers.

After she returned from a maternity leave, she was subjected to belittling, had fingers pointed at her face twinned with the warning "you're not the professional, do as you're told!" She did not get pay increases and was not reclassified.

When a new administrator arrived, Sarah was asked "why are you taking this upon yourself?" Apparently front-line staff members were not supposed to show concern for best practices in the workplace, not even proper sterilization of equipment that could lead to the spread of e-coli if it was not properly sanitized.

She was mocked by her colleagues with statements like "why don't you go work for a hospital?", and "what are you doing back here?"

Sarah describes a "culture of incompetence" and of people "looking the other way" in this nursing home. She says that everyone just "takes the path of least resistance" showing little or no concern for the people for whom they are supposed to be caring. When concerns get raised e-mails are not answered, and reporting of incidents is ignored. It's just the way it is.

The impact for Sarah has also been enormous. She constantly questions herself, worries about the residents who have nowhere to turn, and takes anti-anxiety medication. She is not sleeping very well, and saw a counselor. She finds herself always trying not to offend and is trying to keep her mouth shut, but is then riddled with guilt for saying nothing or defending the practices in the home.

In fact, Sarah is between a rock and a hard place. She must either be true to herself and the people she cares for, or align herself with individuals and a culture of not caring.

So many whistleblowers find themselves in the same situation and many choose to act according to their consciences – something that many others simply do not understand. When self-interest is rampant in a workplace, the people who care about what they do appear as aliens – people from another planet somehow landed on the shores of the workplace. Instead of supporting their attempt at improvement, too often supervisors and co-workers alike attack them, and attempt to bring them down. To them, silence is golden. To whistleblowers silence and having to wrestle with the ravages of their own consciences is worse than death.

The U.K. National Workplace Bullying Advice Line, says that the top reasons for being bullied at work include:

- "being in the wrong place at the wrong time

- being good at your job

- being popular with people

- unwittingly drawing attention to another person's incompetence by simply being competent

- blowing the whistle on malpractice, fraud, illegality, breaches of rules, regulations and procedures, or raising health and safety issues

- having a high level of integrity and emotional maturity."

Since whistleblowers would likely fall into at least four of these categories, it is easy to see why they are more likely to be targeted.

REFERENCES

Anderson, E. (1994). The Code of the Streets. *Atlantic Monthly*, 81-94.

Anderson, J. (May, 2004). Sexual Assault Revictimization. *Research and Advocacy Digest*. 6(3).

Canada Safety Council. (2007). *Bullying in the Workplace.* Retrieved February 26, 2007 from www.safety-council.org/info/OSH/bullies.html

CBC (April 28, 2004). *Whistleblower legislation Bill C-25, Disclosure Protection* Retrieved March 20, 2007 from: http://www.cbc.ca/news/background/whistleblower/

Crick, N.R., Dodge, K.A. (1994). A review and reformulation of social information-processing mechanisms in children's social adjustment. *Psychological Bulletin.* 115(1), 74-101.

Geffner, R., Braverman, M., Galasso, J. Marsh, J. (2004). *Aggression in Organizations: Violence, Abuse, and Harassment At Work And In Schools.* N.Y: Haworth Maltreatment and Trauma Press.

Eggerston, L. (August 31, 2004). Independent Inquiry Needed Into Firing of Whistleblowers. *JAMC*, 171(5) Pg. 438. Retrieved March 20, 2007 from: http://www.cmaj.ca/cgi/reprint/171/5/438.pdf

James,L. R. (1998). Measurement of personality via conditional reasoning. *Organizational Research Methods,* 1, 131-163.

James, L.R., Mazerolle, M.D. (2003). *Personality in Work Organizations* Thousand Oaks, CA: Sage Publications.

Matthiesen, S.B. (2004). When whistleblowing leads to bullying a work. *Occupational Health Psychologist.* 1, 1,3.

O'Leary-Kelly, A.M., Griffin, R.W., Glew, D.J. (1996.) Organization motivated aggression: A research framework. *Academy of Managemen Review.* 21(1), 225-253.

CHAPTER FIVE

Symptoms, Clues, and Warning Signs of Psychological Warfare.

Suddenly work does not seem as much fun. Where you used to look forward to doing your job, you find you can barely drag yourself in to work. You start looking for excuses not to be there. You take your full amount of sick leave, and consider taking a leave of absence to explore other professional possibilities. Your family, friends, and colleagues notice a change in you. You're simply not the enthusiastic person you used to be. Never lacking in confidence, you now find yourself riddled with self doubt, wondering if you even know how to do your job anymore. You feel anxious and uncertain, and tears lie just beneath the surface. You alternate between feeling angry and afraid, but you are not sure what you are afraid of, or at what or whom you should be angry.

If you are a manager, you may have always taken pride in the achievements of your department or area, and your numbers are still pretty good, but the problem is that there appears to be a lot more conflict happening. Team members seem to be at each other's throats. People may have approached you to say that they are no longer satisfied with their positions, their work, or their treatment, and are now seeking transfers out of your jurisdiction. Some simply inexplicably step down from their positions. Others take paid or unpaid leaves, stress leaves, sick leaves. Still others simply quit, citing better opportunities elsewhere. Your best people are leaving and you are getting worried. Furthermore, the behavior of customers, clients, or students appears to be getting more contentious and argumentative.

What may be happening in this situation is that casualties are beginning to return from the front lines of an undeclared psychological war. Fed up with a climate of blame, attack, and hostility, the best and most positive people in a department or organization are likely to be the first to show the strain.

As an organization's climate changes for the worst, it is the positive people in the organization who will feel challenged, attacked, or ignored. When meetings are characterized by blaming behavior, sarcasm, or personal attacks, individuals with any degree of self-esteem will feel the need to flee in order to preserve their positive sense of self. Others will begin to keep their heads down, fearful that if they try to contribute, they will be targeted next. Bright and creative people will stop offering their ideas for fear of being personally attacked, belittled or criticized in private or in front of their peers.

Some managers begin to complain that no one is talking to them. There is a deafening silence pervading the workplace. No one seems to be home. Eventually the problem shows up in the bottom line.

In the interim, people may try valiantly to continue to produce as before, but the stresses and strains begin to show. There is a general feeling that something is terribly wrong. Sometimes the best people just say, as one did recently, that she is looking for other opportunities where she is more likely to have her expertise respected, and that "working here is just too darn hard".

When psychological warfare begins to rear its ugly head at work, individuals begin to experience odd symptoms, and the climate of a workplace can change overnight. Where previously people worked harmoniously and supported each other, now mistrust begins to spread. Where previously there was humor and laughter, now people seem strained.

Employees start "working from home" in order to avoid what is becoming an increasingly unsafe workplace climate. In fact, the office becomes so empty you could shoot a cannonball through it without hitting anyone.

The workplace moves from a culture of acceptance to a culture of shame, blame, and finger pointing. People begin to lunge at each other's throats, and there is constant criticism and nitpicking. People talk about other people behind their backs, criticizing them, making fun of them, blaming them for the problems of the department or organization. There are malicious rumors and vicious innuendo. Individuals are excluded or isolated. They are kept out of the information loop, and are often unaware of a meeting they are supposed to be at. Because of their isolation, they may be unaware of information that is circulating in the organization – information that is vital for them to have in order to do their jobs. Some refuse to attend staff meetings because of the toxic environment. No one seems to understand fully what is going on, but everyone wants something done about it. Nevertheless, few speak up.

People start leaving. Where, before, staff retention was high, now people begin to resign to "seek other opportunities". Not wishing to burn their bridges, few cite the real reasons why they are leaving. Some of the most valued and experienced employees take early retirements. Long and short term disability claims and stress leaves move sharply upward.

Where there was good will, people stop volunteering for duties, saying "it's not my job". Demoralization spreads like a cancer throughout a department or an organization. People stop saying anything, realizing it is not safe to do so, and risk taking, especially at staff meetings is at an all time low. New ideas are not offered. Work is not getting done. Opportunities are lost.

Small groups begin to appear in the lunchroom or around the water cooler, speaking in hushed tones. People exchange knowing looks. Cliques form.

What is often "terribly wrong" is that something has changed. This may occur just after a new employee arrives on the scene, or someone transfers in from another department. A long term employee may feel slighted about something that has not been resolved, and he or she may resort to passive-aggressive behavior in order to get even. There may be a new boss or manager, or someone is promoted into a new position. Since some managers prefer to move their "problem" employees rather than firing them, a new department head inherits the problem, and productivity in her or his department begins to decline.

In a desperate attempt to try to stem the bleeding in a department, a manager may take aim at the likely suspects – those who appear to be behaving negatively. Often this is done without adequate information, or consideration of past performance, an employee's demonstrated abilities, or their character as shown through their previous work history. In doing this, managers may inadvertently punish the very individuals who are targets of workplace warfare. These will be people who have had previously good records, but who are turned off, angry, feeling hurt, victimized, slighted, disrespected and unfairly treated. These may well be the victims, not the perpetrators of workplace warfare. They are reacting to what has happened to them by being defensive, disengaged, and often negative. What occurs next is that the manager may remove them from their areas of responsibility without real cause, thereby making worse the bullying that is already occurring. In some cases, managers may try to get rid of them by constantly changing workplace guidelines or giving them impossible tasks with even worse deadlines, hoping that they will quit.

Managers, not knowing what else to do, may also begin to crack the whip, and demand results, but the results do not come, or there are small gains, then more losses. Others try "professional development" approaches with their employees in a desperate effort to raise morale and productivity, but these efforts do not succeed. Not having addressed the root causes of the problem, educational initiatives are unlikely to go anywhere.

Other managers, in their frustration and anxiety about their department's performance, may become bullies themselves, taking employees to task in front of their peers, yelling, and possibly using profanity. They may engage in constant criticism without any legitimate cause, or belittle an employee's opinions in front of their peers, or subject them to unwarranted punishment. These kinds of actions tend to be both cruel and misguided. If managers are concerned about a climate issue in a department, they would be wise to gather a significant amount of information so that when they do act, they do so based on evidence. It is vitally important for senior managers especially to pay careful attention when a long time employee who has always performed admirably begins to exhibit serious signs of distress, or when other valued employees take early retirement or "stress leave", or ask for transfers.

Pamela worked for a municipality in their social service department. A long time employee with a good track record, like so many others in her area, she was singled out for psychological attack by a new supervisor who was dubbed "the cobra" by employees, for his tendency to attack with little warning.

Her treatment may have been worse because she attempted initially to stand up for co-workers who were also being threatened and mistreated by this individual, and because she was a high achiever, and a very hard worker.

She was repeatedly humiliated in front of her team, and told that if she disagreed with something the supervisor said, perhaps she should get off the team. He regularly made hostile and belittling comments about her to team members and to her superiors. He started rumors and made rude and degrading remarks, attempting to intimidate her in front of others. His behavior was geared toward causing her embarrassment and making her look or feel stupid.

When some of these things worked, he escalated his behavior, telling other staff that they no longer reported to her, effectively removing her job. He tried to replace her with a male with much less experience, and was largely supported in his actions by his male bosses.

This is not an uncommon situation in organizations, where a line manager or supervisor who is attacking an employee that he or she may feel threatened by, actually receives the support of senior management. Sticking to the archaic rule that they must rigidly support their manager over even an employee with an excellent reputation, in order to avoid undermining their supervisor, locks them into a situation where they may be destroying the very culture that produces results. By failing to "walk around" to take stock of, and gain information about what is going on themselves, they inadvertently add to the problem.

Often their best employees leave, and it is not until the bottom line is directly affected by their inability to attract good people, and the loss of their best performers that it finally registers that the problem may not be the employee but the supervisor.

During an important meeting with a government official, Pamela's boss simply did not show up, leaving her to try to explain the situation, then implying that it was she who had made an error about the location. She could not take a day off to go to a doctor's appointment, and she was yelled at, berated, and sometimes threatened in front of others.

The supervisor's behavior seemed paranoid. He would turn off the lights and hide behind two way mirrors and watch people. His actions put service to clients at risk when, to simply demonstrate his power over people, he threatened to close down an entire caseload, and went ahead and moved clients around causing enormous disruption in their lives.

His is a clear example of a "personality disordered" bully, driven by envy, fear, and paranoia making the lives of his employees a living hell. Lacking the ego strength to manage himself, he sought to control others.

When Pamela went to Human Resources begging them to help her, she was discouraged, and told that she could file a complaint but it would likely not go anywhere and her "life would be hell".

The literature on this subject parallels exactly Pamela's experience. Trunk (2006) says that "After you have filed a report, human resources will protect the company, not you. Human Resources executives talk about their concern for harassment. But, according to Jim Weliky of the Boston-based law firm Messing, Rudavsky & Weliky, 'most human resource departments don't live up to their propaganda'. The law is set up to encourage a company to take proscribed steps to protect itself from liability rather than to protect your emotional stability, or, for that matter, your career." Paralleling the advice given to Pamela by HR, Weliky says "Once you take action against a harasser, retaliation is your biggest problem. 'Very few retaliation cases we have were not triggered by reporting the problem to human resources. But not all retaliation is strong enough to make it to court."

Pamela says that she got no assistance from her agency except more threats. No one wanted to admit having made a mistake in hiring this individual, and senior people appeared to simply be trying to cover up their mistake.

She described her life with this supervisor as "constantly dodging bullets" in a metaphoric reference to the psychological war that had been declared on her. She admitted feeling physically threatened because she was "not sure what he was capable of".

Pamela's experience aligns with that of so many others who report that no one in their agency or company helped them. It seemed that they were entirely alone in trying to deter even the most threatening behavior.

In an earlier case, Anne was followed into a washroom and shouted at by a bully. The scenario was reported to both her manager and human resources. Both did nothing, even though the behavior of the supposed professional in question clearly demonstrated a lack of impulse control, no boundaries, and an invasion of privacy. In Pamela's case there were numerous witnesses to her mistreatment, and she had documented evidence that she had asked her harasser to stop, and still management did not act.

Other employees, even those who know what has been occurring, may follow a manager's bad example, taking their cues from her or him. They may begin to sabotage the individual, providing incorrect information or lack of information to make it more difficult for them to perform. They may also begin to pester, stalk, or spy on a targeted employee, or tamper with their belongings or invade their privacy. Or they may just tacitly support the workplace abuse by not coming to the person's aid, or coming forward to advise the manager of the real reasons for problems in the workplace. They are also likely to put on false faces, thanking the manager for new professional development initiatives while knowing that they are futile.

As employees feel more and more insecure in their workplaces, "sucking up" behavior becomes more predominant. False flattery, intended to shore up a manager's flagging ego, further exacerbates the problem, helping the manager to live in a dream world of sorts, unable to get anywhere near what the real problems are.

In Pamela's case her reputation among co-workers was so good that some actually supported her. Nevertheless it took management a long time to finally act.

Workplace bullies will likely feel a sense of satisfaction that they have managed to get others, including the manager, to attack their target as well. They will have succeeded in replicating in their workplaces, what are often dysfunctional power dynamics in their families of origin. These are dynamics that feel familiar and comfortable to them. Their targets, however, experience a very different reality.

Most managers decide not to intervene when psychological warfare is occurring, thinking things will take care of themselves. They almost never do.

Other managers go AWOL, avoiding the workplace altogether, thereby setting a poor example for their employees, and increasing the likeliness that their neglect of their employees will make the problem worse, as employees feel abandoned. Their departments or organizations continue in a downward spiral until someone at the top finally begins to notice that all is not well.

Unfortunately, since few senior managers take the time to walk around and talk with employees, these kinds of problems can continue for lengthy periods of time, until it is almost impossible to address the problem. By then, many valuable employees are lost to the organization. Those who have left badmouth the organization, and soon it has more and more difficulty attracting bright, capable people. Few managers think about the damage done to their organizations when well respected, competent employees leave and tell others about the toxic working conditions.

More importantly, few managers consider the extremely negative impact on the health of their employees of this kind of harassment.

> *The impact on Pamela was enormous. She had to see a psychologist for significant psychological distress. She was placed on medication, and suffered serious pain in her neck. She lost weight and became depressed. She tried everything she knew to stop what was occurring, but in spite of all of her best efforts, she was left feeling, in her words, "like I was going to throw up. I didn't care if a truck hit me". Eventually she went on stress leave.*

So many times the bully in question has a history of completely unprofessional or harassing behavior elsewhere. In Pamela's situation, that was also the case.

> *Her supervisor had a similar history with another agency – one which his new employer had failed to pick up. In speaking with*

those who knew him at his last place of employment, Pamela learned how relieved they all were that they did not have to deal with him anymore, and how sorry they were that she did. By the time he was finally fired, for threatening everyone, including the social services commissioner, the department was in a shambles.

This situation also parallels what happened to Anne, outlined in an earlier chapter. Anne's supervisor did not bother to check her harasser's credentials either, and it was not until Anne spoke with a former co-worker of this individual's that it became clear that she had also engaged in personal attacks and invented accusations against people at her last place of employment.

Thankfully Pamela's colleagues across the province and in her department supported her even though her organization continues to this day not to do so. She stays only because she has a relatively short time to go to retirement. She feels no respect for her superiors and trusts no one, having learned through this horrendously difficult experience that no one was there when the chips were down.

Pamela's experience was similar to Anne's in this regard as well. Anne admitted that after no one in her department offered any visible support while she endured five months of harassment, she has also lost respect for all of them, and trusts no one. Like Pamela, Anne has gone from being a caring and committed employee who once produced strong results and performed well above the call of duty, to someone who is just putting in her time until she can retire and do something "more worthwhile".

This is the high cost that companies, agencies, and organizations pay when they allow the mistreatment of their best employees. The harm to individuals and to organizations is immeasurable.

If these workplace symptoms sound familiar, it is because they are. More and more workplaces are seeing increases in behavior ranging from incivility to outright aggression, along with the accompanying symptoms in employees of frustration, anger, and depression. In the most severe instances, outright violence may be the result.

Transplanted Family Dynamics?

Some believe that the increase in workplace incivility, harassment and warfare begins in families, travels to schoolyards, and if not appropriately addressed, ends up in the workplace, or in the unemployment and welfare lines.

We are all familiar with employees whose prickliness makes them difficult to be around. Co-workers describe having to "walk on eggshells" to avoid offending the person because they seem to take offense at almost everything. They may display a volatility of temperament that is quite frightening to co-workers who try not to offend them, or cause them to feel slighted. This, of course, prevents any degree of honesty from occurring in the workplace, and severely restricts what competent employees are able to do and say. In some ways, individuals who intimidate with their mood swings and harsh behavior hold whole workplaces hostage. Some targets have actually described feeling as if they are in a state of captivity. But more often there is a seething resentment in the workplace that is almost palpable.

We see this in the schoolyard as well. Someone flicks their hair at someone, or looks at them too long, and there is a fight or threats begin to fly. Any small action is interpreted as an offense, and a reason to become aggressive. Kids start keeping their eyes averted and avoid particular individuals so as not to cause an incident.

Sometimes schoolyard bullies graduate to being workplace bullies - yelling, screaming, undermining, gossiping, threatening and pushing their way to the top. When they do not get what they want, or what someone else has, they throw adult temper tantrums. Some resort to physical violence, while others use emotional abuse, making hurtful comments, spreading rumors, or launching false accusations or personal attacks against those they envy. All of this may have originally helped them to survive their dysfunctional families, however, as adults these kinds of behaviors become maladaptive coping strategies that still allow these people to control some others to some degree, but may result in others distancing themselves until the bullies find themselves utterly alone. No one wants to deal with them.

Does the woman whose family was highly critical internalize their critical attitudes and turn them on herself and others, alway trying to be perfect? Does the boy who was always afraid to speak up at home but found other ways to get what he wanted, end up being the passive-aggressive person at the next desk – the one who says things behind your back but denies them when you confront him? Does the frightened child end up as the bullying adult, who gets other employees to gang up on a hapless victim who has inadvertently given offence? How about the younger sibling who was always envious of the older brother or sister against whom his parents unfavorably compared him? Does he take his hatred of high achievers into the workplace? Is the timid woman who sits in the corner cubicle the one using cyberspace and anonymous e-mails to attack your reputation? Barush (2005) has identified "a considerable amount of bullying in e-mail and other communication media leading to negative outcomes regardless of the media utilized."

With schoolyard and Internet bullying now having reached epidemic proportions, are our workplaces likely to become explosive over the next decade? The Toronto Star (Crawford, April 4, 2007:A12) reported that "the anonymity of cyberspace has made it the perfect bullies' tool, so even timid kids, who would never throw a punch, join on-line aggression". Cathy Wing, the education director of the Media Awareness Network claims that it is anonymity that allows this kind of bullying to take place with impunity.

How Bad Families Help To Create Adult Bullies

It is widely recognized in psychological literature that physical, sexual, and emotional abuse can contribute to serious emotional harm, some of which may disrupt interpersonal relationships. Where there are few if any other environmental supports, children, especially those who have endured sustained and multiple types of abuse, may develop serious mental health disorders, including post traumatic stress, depression, anxiety, alcohol and substance abuse as well as a wide variety of other symptoms – all related to early trauma (Richardson, March, 2005). Briere (1992) refers to these as dysfunctional coping strategies. "Adult survivors of maltreatment have been found to engage in certain dysfunctional behavioral patterns, many of which are considered to be coping mechanisms that are used in an attempt to overcome the emotional distress associated with past trauma".

Children who have been bullied or otherwise violated by parents or other caregivers, or siblings, especially those who have been physically abused, have a greater propensity for becoming bullies or victims in their adult lives, sometimes because they misinterpret the actions and motivations of others. "There is much evidence suggesting that physically abused children are more likely to develop aggressive behavior problems. Physically abused children have also been found to be more likely to interpret the actions of their peers as hostile, and to respond inappropriately in an aggressive manner" (Dodge, Bates, & Petit, 1990).

Marital dysfunction, separation, divorce, and domestic violence (Fergusson, Horwood, & Lynskey, 1996), the presence of a step parent (Fleming, Mullen, & Bammer, 1997) where poor attachment may be an issue, and the possible placement of a child in foster care, may also contribute to aggression and interpersonal problems that could lead to either bullying or victimhood in adulthood.

Mullen and Fleming (1998) have said that "child sexual abuse is widely regarded as a cause of mental health problems in adult life". Since we know that individuals who have been sexually abused as children tend to come from disadvantaged and disorganized family backgrounds (Finkelhor & Baron 1986; Beitchman, Zucker, Hood, daCosta & akman, 1991; Mullen, Martin, Anderson, Romans, & Herbison, 1993), these backgrounds may have also contributed to additional risk factors for bullying behavior or victimhood in adult life. Mullen and Fleming (1998) point out that "in some cases, the adverse outcomes attributed to child sexual abuse may be related as much to the disrupted childhood backgrounds, in the context of which the abuse arose, as to the child sexual abuse itself". It is this history of "disrupted childhood backgrounds" that adult harassers and bullies often bring to the work environment. Misinterpreting the actions and motivations of others, or feeling envious and resentful of others, these bullies may regress to where their behavior approximates that of a child fighting her or his way through a dangerous family situation.

Unfortunately, this leaves workplace colleagues at a loss as to how to deal with someone with this kind of history. Since they know from bitter experience that their actions are likely to be misinterpreted, they will usually try to flee the situation – either by disengaging o by physically leaving. This tends to exacerbate the bully's fears of abandonment and raise her or his stress levels, resulting in escalated bullying and aggression.

Even where colleagues have considerable knowledge of family dynamics, as in the social work, psychology, psychiatry, and nursing professions, and understand how to intervene with individuals who are obviously disturbed, they are in a bind. To do so would mean that they are treating colleagues as clients without their permission to do so. This presents an ethical dilemma that places them in an impossible situation professionally.

All of these common family situations can contribute to some individuals becoming bullies in their workplaces. Where the state fails to deal effectively with child abuse and neglect, it pays an economic and psychological price in the schoolyard, the boardroom and elsewhere in the workplace and the larger community.

Woman on Woman And Woman On Man Aggression

Where it used to be believed that males were more likely to be the aggressors, either interpersonally or in the workplace, there is growing evidence that women are developing more aggressive tendencies. Since violent and aggressive girls tend to grow into aggressive and potentially violent women, it is worth taking a look at some of the growing body of literature on aggressive girls.

Girls appear to demonstrate a greater amount of "indirect aggression" (Tremblay, 2000), which is defined as "social" or "relational" aggression, as in shunning, excluding, ignoring, gossiping, spreading false rumors or disclosing another person's secrets" (National Clearinghouse on Family Violence, 2007). This is intended to "disguise hostile intentions to avoid retaliation and social condemnation" (Heim, 2005). These kinds of behaviors in girls often translate into adulthood. "Mean girls grow up to be mean women, make no mistake about that" (Dellasega, 2005:7).

Dellasega (2005:7) describes "relational aggression" as "verbal violence" where words instead of fists are used to inflict damage on other women. "Unlike openly aggressive men, women learn early to go undercover with these assaults. This author describes what often happens between women as "word wars" as women "slay with a smile". She says, "in and out of the workplace as individuals and in groups, these women continue to interact in aggressive ways reminiscent of high school hallways, where girls jockeyed for social status (Dellasega, 2005:8).

Heim (2003) says "it is ironic that on the one hand, when a woman is in emotional pain, she will seek out a female friend for consolation, while on the other, it is often another woman who put her in that predicament in the first place". This kind of behavior is often confusing to male managers who describe it derogatorily as "cat fights". Unfortunately dismissing female on female aggression in a workplace as a "cat fight" is dangerous to the organization as a whole. These "cat fights" can escalate into serious confrontations.

No matter what it is called, it constitutes psychological warfare – one woman attempting to harm or destroy another. Whether it occurs because of women's general feelings of powerlessness or competition for scarce resources in a company, it is extremely harmful to individuals and to organizations.

REFERENCES

1. Barush, Y. (2005). Bullying on the net: adverse behavior on e-mail and its impact. *Information and Management*, 42(2), 361-371.

2. Beitchman, J. H., Zucker, K. J., Hood, J. E., da Costa, G. A. and Akman, D. (1991). A review of the short-term effects of child sexual abuse', *Child Abuse and Neglect*, 15, 537 - 556.

3. Briere, J. (1992). *Child abuse trauma: theory and treatment of the lasting effects.* Newbury Park, CA: Sage Publications.

4. Crawford, T. (April 4, 2007) *Even timid can be nameless bullies on Web, forum told.* The Toronto Star.

5. Dellasega, C. (2005) *Mean girls grown up: Adult women who are still queen bees, middle bees, and afraid-to-be's.* Mississauga, Ont: Wiley.

6. Dodge, K.A., Bates, J.E., and Petit, G.S. (1990). Mechanisms in the cycle of violence. *Science*, 250, 1678-1683.

7. Fergusson, D. M., Horwood, L. J. and Lynskey M. T. (1996). Childhood sexual abuse and psychiatric disorders in young adulthood: Part II: Psychiatric outcomes of sexual abuse. *Journal of the American Academy of Child and Adolescent Psychiatry*, 35, 1365 - 1374.

8. Fleming, J., Mullen, P. E. and Bammer, G. (1997). A study of potential risk factors for sexual abuse in childhood. *Child Abuse and Neglect*, 21(1), 49 - 58.

9. Finkelhor, D. and Baron, L. (1986). *High risk children.* In D. Finkelhor, S. Arajc, A. Browne, S. Peters and G. Wyatt (Eds) *A Sourcebook on Child Sexual Abuse.* Beverley Hills Sage, 60 - 88.

10. Heim, P. (2003). *In the company of women: Indirect aggression among women – why we hurt each other and how to stop.* U.K.: Tarcher.

11. Human Resources Development Canada (1998) *Growing Up in Canada: National Longitudinal Survey of Children and Youth.* Ottawa, ON.

12. Mullen, P.E. & Fleming, J. (Autumn, 1998). Long term effects of child sexual abuse. *Issues in Child Abuse Prevention*, 9. Retrieved May 22, 2007 from: http://www.aifs.gov.au/nch/issues9.html#fam

13. Mullen, P. E., Martin, J. L., Anderson, J. C., Romans, S. E. and Herbison, G. P. (1993). Childhood sexual abuse and mental health in adult life. *British Journal of Psychiatry*, 163, 721 - 732.

14. National Clearinghouse on Family Violence. (2007). *Aggressive girls*. Retrieved August 11, 2007 from: http://www.phac-aspc.gc.ca/ncfv-cnivf/familyviolence/html/nfntsaggsr_e.html

15. Richardson, N. (March, 2005). Social costs: The effects of child maltreatment. *National Child Protection Clearinghouse. Published by: Australian Institute of Family Studies*. Retrieved from: http://www.aifs.gov.au/nch/sheets/rs9.html July 5, 2007.

16. Tremblay, R. (2000). The Origins of Youth Violence. *Isuma*, 1, 2, 19-24.

17. Trunk, P. (February 5, 2006) Don't report sexual harassment (in most cases). *Brazen Careerist*. Retrieved August 20, 2007 from: http://blog.penelopetrunk.com/2006/11/02/dont-report-sexual-harassment-in-most-cases/

18. Weliky, J. (May 2, 2006) *Have a plan to fight workplace harassment*. Quoted by Penelope Trunk. Retrieved August 20, 2007 from: http://www.boston.com/jobs/globe/climb/archives/020506.shtml

CHAPTER SIX

Organizational Vulnerabilities

Are there organizations that are more prone to workplace bullying? Are there aspects of organizational culture and climate that promote attacks by some workers on others, or by some managers on their employees? The literature says that there definitely are factors that help to lay the foundation for bullies to operate with impunity in organizations. Some of these factors have to do with leadership style, job design, organizational norms, values, politics, and communication climates. (Einarsen, Raknes, & Matthiesen, 1994; Vartia, 1996; Zapf, Knorz, & Kulla, 1996; Hoel & Cooper, 2000; Hoel & Salin, 2003).

Some authors see workplace warfare as a symptom of a dysfunctional organization (Baron & Neuman, 1996; Zapf, 1999). Too often though, workplace harassment is simply seen as an unwanted personal characteristic or an example of behavior that is not entirely rational (Salin, 2005), rather than what it is – individuals acting in a way that promotes their own self interests at the expense of others and that harms the organization as a whole.

According to Norm Grosman, a Toronto lawyer, "under common law, a workplace needs to be fair, decent and civil" (O'Brien, 2003). But do most workplaces meet this standard? If not, these organizations are vulnerable to legal action by employees.

Randall (1997:107) says that good managers know very well whether or not the work environment is healthy or "a breeding ground for discontent, hostility and harassment". Managers at all levels are at the very centre of the procedures necessary to minimize harassment and deal with those individuals who are intent upon bullying their fellow employees". Some managers appear unconcerned that there could be repercussions for an organization when they fail to exercise their due diligence requirements to ensure that employees who work for them are safe. In some cases, this lack of concern has been quite costly.

Employees have started to sue organizations when they have failed to protect them from bullying that has led to severe personal consequences. Armour and Hansen (Feb. 10, 1998) report a "flood of retaliation cases surfacing in U.S. workplaces…. In a growing workplace battleground, a record number of employees say they're being fired, demoted and otherwise punished for speaking out against discrimination or harassment. Many are filing lawsuits or complaints against bosses for retaliating against them. Once a fairly rare problem, 'retaliation' charges filed with the Equal Employment Opportunity Commission (EEOC) have more than doubled since 1991 - from 14,708 cases in fiscal 1991 to 31,059 last year. The surge is coming although the overall number of charges filed with the agency has declined since 1997".

Emelise Aleandri and Gloria Salerno successfully sued the City University of New York for one million dollars for bullying suffered at the hands of their supervisor. Constantly subjected to verbal abuse and screaming matches over a period of years, they finally took legal action. After years in the courts, they won (Stuart, May 2005). Theirs is one of many landmark cases now on the books against organizations that fail to take appropriate action to protect their employees from bullying behavior by co-workers, bosses, or clients.

More and more bully prone organizations are being subjected to legal action. "There is a growing tendency for Canadian courts, arbitrators and labor boards to declare the existence of a *duty of fairness* in a variety of legal contexts" according to Health Canada (2006). This duty has been established in a variety of precedent setting cases that include "harassment and discrimination" and "intentional or negligent infliction of nervous shock" (See the cases of Steeves v R. (1995), 11 C.C.E.L. (2d) 112 (F.C.T.D.) and Janzen and Govereau v Platy Enterprises Ltd (1989), 19 C.H.R.R. D/6205) for more information).

According to Health Canada (2006), "these legal developments have created a climate in which high demand/ low control and high effort/low reward conditions — if substantiated by the evidence — could be made the subject of legal actions brought by employees against their employers based on what appears to be an emerging *general* duty of fairness in employment relationships".

What Kind of Organization Creates or Supports Bullies?

There is some evidence that particular kinds of organizational cultures and climates appear to facilitate psychological warfare at work. Namie and Namie (2003) are among several authors who have identified the types of organizational cultures that may inadvertently, or in some cases, deliberately, create workplace bullies. They have identified the following factors that almost guarantee that bullies will operate with impunity in a workplace:

- **"A culture of making the numbers".** Where organizations focus obsessively on "the bottom line" while ignoring the need to foster a workplace where creativity and high levels of production can flourish over the long term, management is ignoring the possibility that the geese that are laying the golden eggs may end up leaving, becoming ill, or dying on the job.

- **Organizations that foster managers who are "ax men or women"** who enjoy firing employees who are not immediately productive, or who have Theory X (authoritarian) management styles, where employees are considered lazy and unmotivated, in need of constant threat of severe consequences for failure to perform, are in serious danger of self destruction. It is unlikely to occur in the short term, but organizations wishing to ensure their continued longevity cannot function as punishment oriented organizations without facing legal consequences as well as threats to their bottom line over time.

- **A focus on individuals' "strength of personality or interpersonal aggressiveness while ignoring emotional intelligence"** is another problem. Emotional intelligence refers to several key characteristics and skills that when present in an organization leads to a healthy climate where creativity and production can remain high. One of these is the "artful critique" where rather than "calling someone stupid or incompetent… ..[the manager] focuses on what a person has done and can do rather than reading a mark of character into a job poorly done" (Goleman, 1995:153). Calling people names is, to put it bluntly, character assassination. It is hurtful, and attacks rather than builds self esteem. Without self esteem, employees are not able to perform up to their level of competence. Employers who lack "the rudiments of emotional intelligence" – the ability to organize groups, negotiate solutions, develop personal connections, and engage in social analysis, in other words "have insights about people's feelings, motives, and concerns", are unlikely to be successful over the longer term. Those who have these qualities are unlikely to allow bullies to function in their organizations for very long.

- **"A focus on short term planning" at the expense of longer term success** is problematic for organizations. Constantly engaging in quick fixes, or putting out fires, encourages a "driver" type of style in organizations, where managers or team leaders push their employees very hard to achieve results, thereby exhausting them, and over time eroding their ability to produce.

- **Where "higher priority [is] given to personal friendships rather than legitimate business interests",** the authors suggest that bullying is more likely to occur. Where personal friendships preclude appropriate action being taken against a manager who maltreats or abuses her or his employees, bullies may be operating freely, wreaking havoc on employees who are afraid to speak up for fear of more professional consequences. A case described earlier – the case of Amelia in Chapter Two, reinforces this. For years, Amelia browbeat, undermined and launched verbal assaults on her employees and other managers, and was allowed to do so with impunity because everyone knew, but no one spoke of her "personal relationship" with the head of the organization. Because she was able to use her sexuality to ensure her position, everyone who dealt with her was unable to confront her, or seek an end to her abusive behavior, fearing repercussions. This kind of situation can poison an organization, and lead to highly dysfunctional dynamics that result in good people leaving, unable to continue to enable a system where secrecy rules, and everyone tiptoes around the obvious.

- **"Frequent misuse of performance appraisal processes and narrowly defined internal conduct codes"** may also contribute to a more bully prone workplace. When performance appraisals are used to target people instead of helping them to grow or become more proficient, bullying is occurring. Where conduct codes are so narrowly defined as to prevent appropriate action being taken against someone whose behavior falls just outside the parameters of the Code, bullying is likely to occur (Namie & Namie, 2003:4).

Interviews with targets turned up a couple of other organizational factors that led to or encourage workplace warfare. A culture of silence and denial, where everyone from the senior managers to front line employees pretend that all is well with the organization when they know it is not, add greatly to the problem. Instead of problem solving, employees and managers in these kinds of organizations stick their heads in the sand and just hope it will all go away. It almost never does. In fact, it gets worse as bullies feel emboldened to act with impunity against their targets.

Babiak & Hare (2006) reinforce the idea that it is exactly these kinds of organizations, ones that are fast paced or undergoing significant change, or living in denial, that may also draw psychopathic personalities, very adept at manipulating others by using charm and clever language, especially with their superiors. In fact, this is an area where senior managers need to pay special attention. Some individuals are very good at flattery, and very adept at slick language and personal presentation. Where senior managers never bother to speak to their employees, or occasionally drop in to see how things are going, they are unlikely to ever know what is really occurring in a department or business unit. Relying only on the accounts of their middle managers to determine what they consider to be the reality of their business, is dangerous. Looking only at numbers is equally dangerous. "Management by walking around" is still the best safeguard against bullying in organizations. Speaking with employees directly will always provide the best information about what may or may not be taking place in an organization.

Some senior managers look the other way when workplace bullies are good at "getting results" from their people through the use of punishment and aversive tactics. Not recognizing that the costs to the organization will be greater in the long run than any short term gain, they are fine with bullying tactics as long as they produce results.

A Negative Corporate Culture and Climate

The Canada Safety Council (2007) has pointed out that a negative organizational culture that creates bullies is sometimes characterized by managers who "expect extra long hours of work on a regular basis, label those who complain as weak or inadequate, and dismiss those who admit to, or show signs of, stress".

Barash (2006) has noted that in a social or corporate culture where opportunities for women are few, lethal competition for scarce resources is more likely to occur. This can lead to woman on woman psychological aggression.

It is this kind of aggression – nasty gossip that is untrue, false rumors circulating, vicious personal attacks, shunning – that may leave male managers utterly flummoxed. Most are unsure of how to handle this kind of behavior and may believe it will simply "blow over". It almost never does.

Managers who fail to address this kind of behavior directly, even if it is denied, are inadvertently encouraging female aggression. The entire goal of this kind of passive-aggressive behavior is to injure the target while remaining below the organizational radar. By addressing the behavior head on and stating that it is unacceptable, managers can greatly reduce it. By examining ways of creating more opportunities for competent women in organizations, managers can sometimes prevent it from occurring in the first place.

Davenport et al (2002: 66, 67) cite the following as some of the reasons why workplace bullying and psychological harassment may flourish in organizations:

- *Poor management practices* – This includes poor communication and problem solving strategies, an "excessive bottom line orientation" that may override "the ethical principle that human resources are a company's most important asset", weak leadership, and little or no teamwork.

- *"A stress intensive workplace"* – Downward and upward mobbing may occur as both workers and supervisors exhibit reactions to constant excessive pressures to produce.

- *"Monotony"* – An absence of challenging, meaningful work can lead to boredom and the possibility of mobbing adding excitement.

- *"Disbelief or denial by managers"* – Perpetuation of mobbing because managers at higher levels do not believe it exists. Denial of serious issues almost always ensure that those issues will explode at some point, and senior management will be forced into damage control mode.

- *"Unethical activities"* – Employees may be mobbed for exposing unethical practices in organizations where there is more concern for the organization's reputation and "the short term bottom line", and less for "the harm it might inflict". Potential difficulties are hushed up, and whistleblowers are scapegoated and silenced. These kinds of organizations are in serious trouble because ultimately they will develop a reputation for lack of ethics and dishonest practices. Once an organizational reputation is lost it is very difficult to regain. Trying to "re-brand" will only go so far in reinstating an organization's reputation. The best practice is to ensure that unethical practices are confronted head on.

- *"Flat organizations"* – "Highly ambitious people who want and need promotions…often resort to techniques that hamper the well being of others" (Davenport et al, 2002:69). Managers at all levels need to watch out for people whose ambitions outstrip their abilities, and who are willing to abuse other people in order to protect themselves or their careers. These are the individuals who, given the right set of circumstances, will become full blown bullies who will injure individuals and the organization given half a chance. The reason is that their concern is not for the well being of the organization, irrespective of what they might say, it is for themselves.

- *"Downsizing, restructuring, mergers"* – "Employees fearing for their jobs might fight for their positions". How change is managed in organizations is critical. Where change is sudden and unannounced, or fails to take into account the need for people to adapt to meet it, or where there is little support for employees who may lose their jobs, there is likely to be the development of a cutthroat culture where people fearing that they may lose their livelihoods, with all the subsequent personal problems that creates, will fight for their professional lives.

Randall (1997) describes the dynamics of oppressive work environments as follows: "Where bullies do thrive in organizations, they do a lot of damage. By making their subordinates scared or intimidated, they put them into a self-protective frame of mind which stifles initiative and innovation. A combination of poor self-esteem arising because the individual victims cannot prevent themselves from being bullied, their feelings of anger at the organization for not properly protecting them, and a great sense of loss of career or the enjoyment of work, conspires to bring down their standards of work.

This can lead to a strange quirk of fate - the bully who continues to perform well is then seen as being surrounded by less competent people and is more likely to be promoted than they are" (Randall, 1997:51).

This is one of those ironic twists that occurs where bullies function without restriction in organizations, and where senior managers may be out of touch with what is really occurring in individual departments. The wrong people will get promoted, and the organization will suffer as a result.

A Symptom of Organizational Dysfunction?

Other authors have shown that workplace warfare is often declared in organizations that, like failed states, are unable to produce, or even protect their corporate citizens. These organizations tend to be characterized by:

- Role conflict

- Lack of control over work

- Heavy workloads

- Organizational restructuring

- Changes in management

- Negative management styles (either too autocratic or too laissez-fair with weak leadership and vague supervision)

- A problematic climate (unwelcoming, unfriendly, and not supportive).

Keashly and Jagatic (2003) complete the list of organizational symptoms by stating that organizations where teamwork is not encouraged, where there is a lack of employee involvement in decision making, where morale is low, and positive supervision almost non-existent are also often organizations where "a permission to harass" exists and may be encouraged as "functional" by management (Brodsky, 1976).

Leymann (1993) adds that the four major factors that appear to lead to workplace warfare are: deficiencies in work design, weak leadership, low moral standards in a department or departments, and leaving particular individuals "socially exposed" by failing to intervene when targets are attacked.

Some authors have pointed out that where a workplace is highly competitive rather than collaborative, and where stress levels are high, there is more likely to be bullying and other types of conflict (O'Moore, Seigne, McGuire & Smith, 1998). These types of organizations also tend to be characterized by co-workers competing for favor among bosses (Einarsen, 2000).

The Special Case of Academia

While post-secondary education may not be the only sector where bullying and harassment exist, it may well be among the worst. In the thousands of mobbing case studies that Leymann carried out, universities were among the most highly represented workplaces (Chronicle of Higher Education, April 14, 2006). There are several organizational reasons for this, chief among them, the changing academic environment.

MaGregor et al (2006) say that "As public sector organizations, universities face increased pressure to conform to a 'business ethic' and many of the consequences are likely contributory factors of workplace bullying. The loss of middle managers and other personnel trained in conflict resolution, reduction of internal job ladders and other mechanisms providing job security, a tendency towards autocratic managerial styles etc" all contribute to a negative climate and culture. This movement to more of a "business model" may well be eroding the collegial spirit that once characterized institutions of higher learning.

This should be of concern to the social science, health care, and business sectors of the economy. Where universities and colleges no longer offer the opportunity to think and speak freely, students are being shortchanged, and creative ideas are being suppressed.

Modern business leaders understand how important it is to recruit creative people who are capable of weighing options and developing innovative solutions to business problems. Everyone loses when the capacity to develop these kinds of innovators at the post-secondary level is lost. Where professors and post-secondary administrators model inappropriate behavior for students, they are likely to take what they have learned into the workplace.

Stark (1996) has argued that competition is a significant feature of academic environments. This might include competition to achieve enrolment numbers, professional recognition, to meet organizational expectations concerning student feedback, the development of new curriculum and programs, and in achieving superior academic success through research or other professional activities. With competition comes some risks. In examining competition in a variety of fields, Gorney and Long (1980) found that it is associated with psychological and physical aggression and hence psychological distress and subsequent mental health problems, and is not associated in either direction, positively or negatively, with achievement. Nevertheless, competition is both tacitly and openly rewarded in many academic institutions.

Stark (1996) is blunt in his assessment of the academic environment He believes that psychological violence is not only condoned but rewarded. Perpetrators are also unlikely to change since they have benefited and may continue to do so in this type of system, leading to the maintenance of a destructive status quo. .

He sees lying as another feature of academia, and considers the generation of false rumors to be one of the most insidious forms o lying. False rumors are particularly harmful in academic settings where the rumor mill works overtime, because often the target of the rumors is unaware of them, and is unlikely to be believed or seen as defensive if s/he attempts to dispel them. The "where there's smoke, there's fire" view is widespread, even in academia, and it rarely occurs to people who have not been affected, that perhaps the rumors and the attempts to dispel them were both caused by a "psychological arsonist". When left unchecked rumor mongering can lead to two additional problems - the victim may be labeled a pariah, and others fear coming to her or his defense in case they are "tarred with the same brush". Once the intended target has become isolated in this way, the field is left open for the bully to continue her or his attacks.

Mobbing appears also to be common in post secondary environments. Leymann, a German psychologist, first coined the term in the 1980's and defined it as "an impassioned, collective campaign by co-workers to exclude, punish and humiliate a targeted worker" (Chronicle of Higher Education, April 14, 2006). The problem is particularly prevalent in post secondary institutions. Westhues has seen mobbing as more likely to occur in universities because tenure creates high job security, because there are "few objective measures of performance", and because there is "frequent tension between loyalty to the institution and loyalty to some higher purpose". He says that the danger in post secondary education is to "think we're above all that", and deny or minimize the problem.

The Canadian Association of University Teachers (2006) sees the following as possible contributors to workplace violence in higher education, including bullying and harassment: "job loss or insecurity, overcrowded classes, lack of resources or personal issues can cause people to lash out. Fear of failure, both on the part of staff and students, mental illness, low self esteem and a need to control are other examples. Loss of control over the work environment and the ensuing fallout often leave staff feeling helpless and undervalued.

One of the biggest contributing factors may be the employer's lack of awareness and attention to staff morale and a true grasp of the day-to-day needs and dynamics within the university setting. Trying to meet the bottom line can cause resentment, hostility, and paranoia amongst otherwise healthy individuals".

Whether or not psychological warfare occurs in health care, social services, business, industry, or academic settings, it is often preceded by specific organizational factors. By addressing these root causes, managers can begin to change corporate cultures and create more wholesome climates where work is more likely to get done.

REFERENCES

Armour, S., Hansen, B. (Feb. 10, 1998). U.S. workplace becomes battleground. *USA Today.*

Babiak, P., Hare. R.D. (2006). *Snakes in suits: When psychopaths go to work.* N.Y.: HarperCollins.

Barash, S. (2006) *Tripping the prom queen: The truth about women and rivalry. NY:* St. Martin's Press.

Baron, R.A. & Neuman, J.H. (1996) Workplace violence and workplace aggression: Evidence on their relative frequency and potential causes. *Aggressive Behavior,* 22, 161-173.

Brodsky, C.M. (1976) *The harassed worker.* Toronto: Lexington Books.

Canada Safety Council. (2007) *Employers: What you need to know about bullying in the workplace.* Retrieved July 14, 2007 from: http://www.alis.gov.ab.ca/tips/archive.asp?EK=11594

Chronicle of Higher Education. (April 14, 2006). *Mob rule: In departmental disputes, professors can act just like animals.* Retrieved February 5, 2007 from: http://chronicle.com/free/v52/i32/32a01001.htm

Coyne, I., Seigne, E, Randall, P. (2000) Predicting workplace victim status from personality. *European Journal of Work and Organizational Psychology,* 9(3), 335-349.

Davenport, N., Schwartz, R.D., Elliott, G.P. (2002). *Mobbing: emotional abuse in the American workplace.* Ames, Iowa: Civil Society Publishing.

Einarsen, S. (2003). Harassment and bullying at work: A review of the Scandanavian approach. *Aggression and Violent Behavior.* 4(5), 379-401.

Einarsen, S., Raknes, B.I., Matthiesen, S. (1994). Bullying and harassment at work and their relationships to work environment, quality: an exploratory study. *European Work and Organizational Psychologist,* 4(4), 381-401.

Goleman, D. (1995) *Emotional Intelligence.* N.Y.: Bantam.

Gorney, R. & Long, J.M. (1980). Cultural determinants of achievement, aggression, and psychological distress. *Archives of General Psychiatry, 37,* 452-459.

Health Canada (2006) *Environmental and Workplace Health.* Retrieved February 5, 2007 from: http://www.hc-sc.gc.ca/ewh-semt/pubs/occup-travail/work-travail/stress-part-1/illness-maladie_e.html#employers

Hoel, H., Cooper, C. (2000). *Destructive conflict and bullying at work.* Manchester School of Management. University of Manchester Institute of Science and Technology, Manchester.

Hoel, H., Salin, D. (2003). *Organizational antecedents of bullying.* In *Bullying and Emotional Abuse in the Workplace: International Perspectives in Research and Practice.* S. Einarsen, H. Hoel, D. Zapf, C. Cooper (Eds), 203-218. London: Taylor & Francis.

Keashly, L., Jagatic, K. (2003). *By another name: American perspectives on workplace bullying.* In S.Einarsen, H. Hoel, D. Zapf & C.L. Cooper (Eds). *Bullying and emotional abuse in the workplace,* 31-61. London: Taylor & Francis.

Leymann, H. (1993). *Mobbing – Pscyhoterror am arbeitsplatz und we man sich dagegen wehren kan.* Hamburg: Powolt Reinbeck.

MaGregor, M.W., Quinlan, E., Joyce, G., Watkinson, A. (2006). *Bullying and mental health in academic workplaces: The problem and the solution.* Canadian Institute of Health Research. Institute of Neurosciences, Mental Health and Addiction.

Mattheisen, S.B. (2006) *Bullying at work: Antecedents and outcomes* University of Bergen, Norway. Retrieved August 20, 2007 from https://bora.uib.no/bitstream/1956/1550/6/Mainthesis_Matthiesen.pdf

Namie, G & Namie, R. (2003). *The bully at work.* Naperville, Illinois Sourcebooks Inc.

O'Brien, S. (2003). *Invisible attacker.* Capitalnewsonline. Carleton University, School of Journalism.

O'Moore, M., Seigne, M., McGuire, L., Smith, M. (1998). Victims of bullying at work in Ireland. *Journal of Occupational Health and Safety – Australia and New Zealand.* 14(6), 569-574.

Randall, P. (1997). *Adult bullying: Perpetrators and victims.* London & New York: Routledge.

Salin, D. (November, 2005). Workplace bullying among business professionals: prevalence, gender differences and the role of organizational politics. *Pistes* 7(3) Swedish School of Economics and Business Administration.

Stark, C. (1996). *Psychological violence in academia.* Canada: University of Regina. Retrieved February 20, 2007 from: http://uregina.ca/~starkc/psychological_violence_in_academia.html

Stuart, C. (May, 2005). HEO lawsuit nets $1million. *Clarion. Newspaper of the professional staff congress.* City University of New York.

Vartia, M. (1996). The sources of bullying: psychological work environment and organizational climate. *European Journal of Work and Organizational Psychology,* 5(2), 203-214.

Zapf, D. Einarsen, S. (2005). *Mobbing at work: Escalated conflicts in organizations.* In. S. Fox, P.E. Spector (Eds) *Counterproductive work behavior,* 237-270. Washington, DC: American Psychological Association.

Zapf, D. (1999). Organizational work group related and personal causes of mobbing/bullying at work. *International Journal of Manpower,* 20(1,2), 70-85.

Zapf, D., Knorz, C., Kulla, M. 1996). On the relationship between mobbing factors and job content, social work environment, and health outcomes. *European Journal of Work and Organizational Psychology,* 5(2), 215-237.

CHAPTER SEVEN

What Managers Need To Know

There are three things that managers most need to know about psychological warfare in the workplace – its symptoms, how it affects their employees, their departments and the organization, and what they can do about it.

Many managers find this a very difficult issue to address in the workplace. It is made more difficult by "s/he said s/he said" situations, employees' silence and inability or refusal to discuss the issue, by the shame felt by those being targeted, and by the cleverness of workplace harassers. Sometimes managers can be targeted as well by more senior managers or by those who report to them.

In this chapter several ways that managers can more effectively address this problem will be outlined.

It Starts With Hiring

One way that harassers and bullies make their way into workplaces is by carefully concealing their negative employment histories and unwanted personality traits. Even personality disordered bullies can conceal their antisocial behavior in a single interview. Those who forge their credentials, or embellish their abilities, can sometimes slip things by in one interview, especially if their references are not carefully checked.

Harassers often rely on their "gift of the gab" to "make friends" with interviewers, coming across as likeable and affable, easy going, and competent, when in fact, they are anything but. Even the best and most experienced interviewers can be fooled by practiced liars. Psychopathic bullies pride themselves on their ability to confuse and mislead interviewers – taking advantage of other people is part of their lifestyle.

Busy managers who do not take the time to carefully check not only someone's credentials, but their claimed accomplishments, and how well they would fit in, will sometimes pay the price in having hired a bully who later makes their lives miserable.

Randall (1997:108) has pointed out the "haste makes waste" phenomenon in employee hiring saying that "all too often people with quite antisocial personalities have been welcomed into the organization by selection teams made up of individuals who have not been fully committed to the process. Frequently they are uninterested in the interpersonal relationships between staff and narrow mindedly look for applicants to fulfill specific functions only." It is the impact on a team of this kind of personality that "often leads to the fragmentation of those teams because the people selected bring with them an agenda for domination and the abuse of power".

Mistakes in hiring can be costly. The more that is invested up front in the hiring process, the less likely that a manager will be sorry later for having made a dreadful mistake.

Avoid Hiring By Single Interview

A single interview is generally not the best way to hire staff. It is also dangerous to assume that any one manager knows best when making hiring decisions. Multiple interviews are often necessary so that more opinions can be sought. Team interviews or tasks as part of the interviewing process are vital. Setting up a practice work situation involving a team, and then seeking their opinions afterwards about whether or not they can work with the person would be helpful. Mixed feelings or negative feedback from trusted team members should be carefully considered, and checked out in second or even third interviews. Goodness of fit may, in some cases, be more important than a person's qualifications and experience.

In conducting interviews be sure to:

- Always ask the employee why they are leaving or have left their current position;

- Get specifics concerning the applicant's experience and academic qualifications – do not accept general answers. If you are unsure of what the applicant means, ask her/him for more detail and check for avoidance behavior;

- Test out the person's skills by asking her/him a few skill testing questions;

- Check out the applicant's credibility by asking her/him who can confirm or may have more direct knowledge of their stated accomplishments;

- Ask some questions that test the individual's deductive reasoning ability (the candidate's ability to apply recognized facts to new situations to reach a conclusion, or the ability to use logic in thinking through a problem);

- Provide a test of an individual's written communication skills;

- Ask the candidate to comment on the main points of something you ask them to read, to test for reading comprehension;

- Check the individual's general literacy by asking her/him something about what s/he enjoys reading, then ask the person to comment on what they enjoyed about it. (Perrin & DeDominic, 2007).

- Ask "how, what, which, when, and who" questions to solicit details;

- Ask "compare and contrast" questions such as "Tell us about a time you feel that you performed well and contrast that with a time you feel that you did not, and discuss a bit about the differences between the two"'.

- Check the person's ability to explore options by asking her or him an "options" question, such as providing a case scenario and asking about what options the person feels s/he may have in this situation;

- Ask a question where the person may be required to explore a differing viewpoint such as "Tell me about a time when you disagreed with a colleague. Why do you believe s/he took the position that s/he did?";

- At some point during the interview, provide constructive but negative feedback to see how well the person can accept criticism.

Perhaps most importantly, do not rely only on your impression of a candidate in a formal interview. Try to establish a less formal interview at a later date, say a luncheon, or off site coffee meeting with at least one other person present. Where possible, as discussed earlier, try to involve a work team in evaluating the candidate.

When hiring senior managers, it may be necessary to use a special psychological test, or at the very least "personality profiling" to screen for possible psychopathy or other negative character traits. Babiak and Hare (2006) in their book, "Snakes In Suits", say that individuals with psychopathic personalities tend to be drawn to positions of power and influence.

Recent events in the corporate world where formerly successful businesspeople have found themselves behind bars for grossly unethical and criminal conduct that in some cases led to the collapse of their companies, underscores the need to be extremely careful in hiring very senior managers. Enron, Worldcom, Hollinger, and OneTel all come to mind as examples where managers who had no qualms about fraudulent practices or outright theft functioned with impunity to the severe detriment of their companies and those who invested in them.

Drs. Babiak and Hare describe these types of individuals as "social psychopaths", unbothered by ordinary "social anxieties", looking for corporate "feeding grounds". To combat what appears to be a significant and growing problem in the corporate world, they have developed the Business Scan 360 (B Scan 360) to screen out possible corporate psychopaths - individuals who display a degree of callousness, manipulativeness and superficial charm well above the norm. Psychopathic individuals' limbic systems tend not to respond normally to other's distress, and this allows them to manipulate, exploit and harm other people with impunity (Management Issues, May 5, 2005). Their test is based on personality profiles of "corporate leaders" convicted of crimes like fraud or embezzlement and involves a 360 degree examination of future corporate leaders before hiring takes place (Management Issues August 20, 2004; BBC News, December 1, 2004).

Unfortunately, according to research conducted by another psychologist, Dr. John Clark, employers may not only be failing to screen for psychopathic behavior, they may in some cases be "actively selecting them" (Management Issues, May 5, 2005). Some job advertisements that are seeking someone who will "do whatever it takes" to get the job done, or want someone who "likes to win" may, in fact, be attracting psychopathic individuals. Unfortunately, employers who are seeking individuals with these kinds of traits may find somewhere down the line, much to their shock, that the psychopath has them in her or his sights, because s/he wants their position and is willing to "do whatever it takes" to get it. Any employer who believes that she or he can "control" a psychopathic employee may be living in a fool's paradise. The best option is to take the necessary steps to try to prevent their infiltration of the workplace.

Conduct Thorough Background Checks

Thorough background checks are necessary <u>before</u> interviews take place, keeping in mind that references may be less than helpful if another organization is eager to rid itself of a troublesome employee (Randall, 1997:109). Generally speaking, professional references are more useful than personal ones. Make sure you check at least three references. If someone is claiming professional, trade, or academic qualifications, check to ensure that their credentials are valid. If someone belongs to a professional College or other professional body, contact them to ensure that the candidate's record is clean. You may want to ask an applicant to sign a release allowing you to ask detailed questions of references and to check their academic and professional qualifications.

Look for:

- Whether or not an employee lists her or his previous supervisor or manager as a reference or only co-workers or others in her/his professional reference list;

- If no previous manager or supervisor is listed, ask why;

- Ask the individual why they selected these people as references and what they believe they can tell you about the person's background and work history;

- In calling references, always ask them about accomplishments the person is alleged to have had, getting specifics of what role the individual played in achieving the results s/he is claiming;

- If you have a question about the candidate arising from their resume or how they performed in an interview, ask the reference for their impressions or any information they can provide related to your question;

- Ask references why the person left, and if they would hire the person back if they had the chance;

- Ask how strongly they would recommend hiring the person;

- Pay attention to neutral or half hearted responses and probe more deeply into those answers;

- Confirm the length of time the person was employed, and other basic employment facts, and ask about whether or not s/he ever reported to other supervisors;

- Ask the applicant if s/he would mind if you also spoke with the other supervisors;

- Use indirect references as well if you know someone who may have previously worked with the individual. Without giving away the information that someone has applied for a job, you can ask people who know the person if they ever worked with them;

- When hiring very senior people, Babiak and Hare's (2006) B Scan 360 screening tool for psychopathy may be helpful.

As Randall (1997: 108) says: "Prevention is generally better than cure, and this is certainly the case when good employment selection procedures can help to keep bullies out of the workforce."

Diagnosing Organizational Issues By Cue and Symptom

Every organization offers important internal cues and symptoms of what may or may not be occurring. A manager's ability to "diagnose" and act on these cues and symptoms may mean the difference between a healthy, happy place to work, and one that is beset by psychological warfare.

Symptoms of workplace warfare have been discussed earlier, but this checklist of possible symptoms may be helpful for managers who believe that their department or organization may be being affected by a workplace bully.

The Canada Safety Council (2005) lists the following red flags that may be symptoms of psychological warfare at work:

- Employees suddenly performing poorly, lower quality, and deadlines not met

- Increases in absenteeism and higher employee turnover

- Plummeting morale

- Bullied employees retaliating against others by sabotaging work, and failing to meet quotas or deadlines

- Decisions being made that harm the organization

- Increases in injury or unsafe behavior

- Higher workloads for co-workers because of a bully's or target's underperformance

- Higher costs for employee assistance programs, and short and long term disability claims

- Having to spend money to replace employees who have left because of psychological warfare.

I would add:

- Requests for transfers out of a department

- Increased stress leaves and early retirements

- Increased use of sick days and other absences

- Formerly competent employees becoming surly, uncommunicative, and turned off

- Infighting, backstabbing, shaming, blaming, and criticism

- Silence and lack of communication – of ideas, concerns, possibilities

- Passive-aggressive behavior – lateness, lack of follow-through, behavior designed to deliberately frustrate the work of the department

- People walking on eggshells to avoid a moody or temperamental employee or supervisor.

Sometimes the types of illnesses that an individual or groups begin displaying may point to psychological warfare. Some physical and emotional symptoms may include:

- Higher levels of stress and anxiety

- Withdrawal and isolation, just wanting to be left alone

- Sudden weight gain or loss

- Listlessness, and extreme tiredness

- Low affect – expressionless face, depressed demeanor

- Uncharacteristic anger or irritability

- Complaints about physical aches and pains, headaches, gastrointestinal problems

- Employees seeming overly vigilant to the point of paranoia

- Lack of concentration and focus

- Sudden self-doubt and lack of confidence in a formerly confident employee

- An employee who looks like they are not sleeping well.

All of these may be indicators that something is amiss and are worth exploring in a supportive way with the employees affected. Since many employees will not want to '"badmouth their boss or co-workers" for fear of professional repercussions, it will be important to approach their obvious distress in a sensitive way, attempting to make them feel comfortable to talk about what is upsetting them.

In Gathering Information

In all of the above instances it is important for managers to act quickly to determine what is happening and why. The best way to achieve this is to gather information, and this can be done in several ways:

- In their book, "In Search of Excellence" Peters and Waterman (2004) coined the term "management by walking around". Managers need to leave their offices and drop in on employees, asking them how things are going, what they are working on, and how they are feeling about the workplace and their jobs. Invitations to speak up may yield valuable information. Employees who hint at something wrong should be encouraged to drop in for a chat with a specific invitation to "call my secretary and book a time to meet".

- Begin appearing at staff meetings and other departmental events. Talk with people before and afterwards. Watch the dynamics that occur in these meetings to determine what kinds of communications occur and what the quality of relationships between individuals are. Who are the formal and informal leaders?

- Make time to talk with both the formal and informal leaders about what you observed and check out their perceptions.

- Ask human resources to flag any departments where absenteeism, leaves, early retirements, or people stepping down from their positions or quitting seem to be a problem. Call in the department head and ask her or him about the number of individuals who seem to be ill or leaving. Conduct confidential exit interviews with those who have left. Call those on sick leave at home to ask about how they are doing and engage them wherever possible.

- Cultivate "bellweathers". Organizational bellweathers – individuals with excellent track records who have demonstrated their ability to produce good results and have shown loyalty to the company or organization should be encouraged to drop in, or chat on a regular basis. Their opinions should be sought about how well the organization is running, what could be improved and their ideas on how this could be accomplished. These individuals should be regularly reminded of how valuable they are to the organization.

- Identify who is in charge of what is not working, and begin to query her or him on your concerns and what actions s/he sees as appropriate under the circumstances. Where actions do not seem appropriate begin to coach the individual in how to confront the problems.

- Take a hard look at the organizational culture and determine whether or not the organizational factors that promote workplace warfare as described in Chapter Six apply. If so, begin to dismantle the organizational precursors to bulling behavior.

In Changing The Climate and Culture of The Organization

Most studies of workplace harassment say that the issue comes down to respect – respect for self and co-workers. Recognition of how each person's behavior affects another is paramount to preventing psychological harassment and the escalation, hurt feelings, and hurt careers that often come with it. But how can managers begin to change the culture and climate of their organizations? Much has been written about this subject, but here are some practical suggestions of immediate steps that managers can take to turn their corporate culture and climate around.

- Expectations concerning respectful behavior in the workplace should be distributed widely.

- Employees' roles and how they go about their jobs should be clarified.

- Regularly seek employees' input and feedback concerning organizational goals and possible methods of achieving them.

- Avoid a too rigid adherence to organizational structure - make it clear that employees are welcome to talk at any time with senior management rather than just reporting through their direct supervisors and managers.

- Follow up on employee suggestions with supervisors in a sensitive way by using phrases that begin "I wonder i this might be a possibility?", and seeking the supervisor' input.

- Pay special attention to the interpersonal dynamics in team meetings. Follow up with direct supervisors, sharing what you noticed, and discussing with them what steps they might take to correct destructive or dysfunctional means of communication.

- Recognize and reward pro-social and respectful formal and informal leadership through promotions, awards, raises, and more resources. This sends a message to an entire organization that those who get along while producing results will reap the benefits.

- Display excitement and interest in what people in the organization or department are doing by giving positive verbal comments and/or sending notes to them congratulating them on a job well done.

- Take immediate and visible action to deal with harassment and bullying by meeting with the alleged target and harasser and gathering the facts.

- Interviews with an alleged harasser should include clear instruction concerning the expectations that the manager has for the ways that the individual will interact with others.

- Graduated consequences should result for bullying and harassing behavior and these should be implemented quickly where thorough investigation and interviews with the alleged harasser and target, as well as others on a team reveal a problem.

In Taking Action –Progressive Discipline

Different jurisdictions have differing requirements concerning graduated discipline for workplace behavior and results that do not meet the requirements of the employer. These may also differ depending upon whether or not there is a collective agreement in place in a workplace, in which case employers and employees are required to live by the provisions of that agreement.

Generally speaking, the following will be helpful for managers having to discipline an employee for bullying or harassing other employees, whether or not there is a collective agreement in place.

After meeting with an employee to set out clear expectations with respect to the way that they treat their fellow employees, it is wise for managers to document the date, time and place as well as the nature of the discussion and the employee's responses. Some managers may wish to negotiate specific goals and methods for addressing them with an employee and outline them in a special agreement, which is signed by the employee. Whether or not this is possible will depend upon employment standards legislation and any collective agreement affecting the workplace.

Written Warning for Unsatisfactory Job Performance

Should meeting with an employee accused of harassment not obtain the desired results, the next step would be to issue a written warning to the employee that is sent to their home by registered mail and also placed in their employment file. This is usually preceded by a meeting wherein the manager would:

- Review with the employee the previous discussion concerning their agreement to change specific behavior related to fellow employees;

- Discuss in concrete terms, the ways in which the employee has not met the manager's stated expectations, giving specific examples wherever possible;

- Ask the employee why these expectations have not been met;

- Indicate that a letter will be placed in the employee's file and discuss any other consequences related to their continued underperformance;

- State what will happen next should the unacceptable behavior continue.

Letters of warning should, in the first sentence, state that this is a written warning concerning the employee's job performance, briefly summarize previous discussions concerning the areas where the manager asked the employee to improve and what improvements were required, outline the ways in which the employee has not met the required expectations, reiterate what specific changes are necessary and within what timeframe, and indicate what consequences will follow should the employee continue not to meet behavioral expectations. Most managers will also include a brief statement of an employee's rights to appeal.

What Next?

Should an employee continue to harass or bully fellow employees, the manager has a couple of additional options that should be exercised before employment is terminated.

The manager may decide to issue a second warning letter much like the first, but adding that continued failure to change behavior could result in an employee's dismissal. Or the manager could issue a second warning letter and follow it up with either a short or longer term suspension without pay, depending upon the severity of the behavior. Generally speaking, a suspension of whatever length without pay requires more senior level approval. Many organizations also require that managers considering suspension discuss how this would be done with the Human Resources department to ensure proper compliance with the organization's HR policies. In some cases organizations allow pre-suspension hearings with the employee and their representative, the manager, and someone from HR, or a more senior manager, prior to a suspension without pay taking place.

Should the behavior continue beyond a second warning letter and / or suspension, the employee may be demoted, subject to further suspension, or have their employment terminated, depending upon what was stated in previous warnings, as well as the severity of the behavior. Demotions or terminations are generally subject to more senior level approval, and are often accompanied by a lawyer drafted letter of termination.

Managers would be wise to consult with HR prior to dismissing an employee. In many cases a resignation can be negotiated without dismissal having to take place. Most employees prefer not to "burn their bridges" by having to leave without letters of reference, or out of concern about being "badmouthed" if they work in a particular industry where managers know each other.

Offering an employee an honorable way out is usually a sound practice, however, this is not always possible. In instances where other workers feel unsafe, it may be wiser to have the individual escorted to the door by security, and their personal effects delivered to their homes.

In severe cases "no contact" orders may be issued. This can be done through a lawyer's letter, or by seeking a restraining order through the courts. This may be done where there is concern about possible violent reprisal, and allows the police to place the person under arrest for breaching the terms of the order.

In cases involving employees engaged in psychological warfare at work, it is often wiser to terminate the employee with pay in lieu of notice to avoid having an angry employee onsite for the notice period. In very severe cases where threats have been made or an assault has taken place, employers may decide to simply dismiss an employee without pay or notice. Even these dismissals with cause, often result in lawyer negotiated outcomes where some payment is made.

In Implementing Softer Solutions To Prevent or Address Workplace Warfare

Justice Canada's report <u>Towards a Workplace Free of Conflict and Harassment</u> contains several helpful suggestions for workplaces wishing to minimize psychological harassment, including the need for all employees, managers and those who report to them, to be aware of what impact their behavior and comments have on others. Other's reactions are important gauges of this. Where injury is done, an apology should be offered (Justice Canada, 2001).

Some of the rights and responsibilities of managers in maintaining a civil workplace culture may include:

- Modeling appropriate behavior by exercising their own authority in a respectful manner and setting a good example;

- Ensuring that their own instructions to employees are clear and establishing fair policies for assigning work, evaluating employees' performance, and enforcing discipline;

- Spelling out what type of behavior is accepted in the workplace and what is not, perhaps in a Code of Conduct, and establishing a clear protocol for investigating complaints concerning bullying and harassment;

- Making sure that employees are made aware of how to prevent and resolve conflicts in the workplace, and how to make formal and informal complaints concerning harassment.

- Where harassment appears to be occurring, either moving in immediately to establish clearer expectations and outlining possible consequences, or obtaining the assistance of a third party to do so.

Blake, Cassels and Graydon law firm say that the following principles should guide manager's decisions as they address any disciplinary action, including psychological harassment. "Discipline must be administered in a way that will not subject the employee to humiliation, disrespect or contempt".

- "Disciplinary measures should be designed to give notice to an employee that behaviour is not acceptable but also that he or she can remedy the situation by following certain rules or guidelines.

- An offer to provide training or guidance may demonstrate the good faith motives of the employer.

- An employer should not tolerate aggressive behaviour or derogatory comments by supervisors or managers.

- If employees in one department receive a disproportionate number of disciplinary measures, employers should be wary of supervision problems.

- A clear written policy on psychological harassment may help to deter some potential harassment "offenders".

- Supervisors and management should be given training or refresher courses on acceptable methods of meeting and communicating with employees having problems.

- Beware of conflicts between co-workers. The employer must provide a work environment free of harassment and management must intervene where there are problems between co-workers.

- Employers should take time to fully assess a situation before subjecting an employee to drastic disciplinary measures. If an employee has not responded to previous measures, there may be underlying problems worth investigating.

- Problems involving employees who have recently returned from a leave of absence should be treated with caution. The productivity of these employees may be impaired by changes in work methods or tools while on leave. Additional training may be required".

It is important to address the matter of workplace warfare early on. Allowed to fester, it will be much more difficult to address as time goes on. Employees must not get the message that bullying and harassment are tolerated within the organization, and the easiest way to prevent this is to act early and effectively to stop it.

Managers can contribute to a healthy and productive work environment by not avoiding issues concerning workplace disrespect and harassment when they arise. Frank communication about the appropriateness or inappropriateness of a particular course of conduct is required for employees to recognize what the organizational culture will and will not tolerate. Employees take their cues from managers, and therefore it is incumbent upon managers to treat employees with respect, thereby setting the standard for a cooperative workplace.

REFERENCES

Babiak, P. & Hare, R.D. (2006). *Snakes in suits: When psychopaths go to work*. N.Y.: HarperCollins

Blake, Cassels, and Graydon (November, 2004). *New Prohibitions Against Psychological Harassment in Quebec*. Retrieved July 16, 2007 from: http://blakes.com/english/publications/leb/Nov2004/NewProhibitions.asp

BBC News (December 1, 2004). *Spotting Psychopaths At Work*. Retrieved July 15, 2007 from: http://news.bbc.co.uk/2/hi/uk_news/northern_ireland/4057771.stm

Canada Safety Council. (2005). *Bullying in the Workplace*. Retrieved February 20, 2007 from: www.safety-council.org/info/OSH/bullies.html

Employers' Law. (March 2, 2006). *Put the bullies on the back foot*. Retrieved February 20, 2007 from: http://www.personneltoday.com/Articles/2006/03/02/33208/Put+the+bullies+on+the+back+foot.htm

Justice Canada (2001). *Towards a workplace free of conflict and harassment*. Retrieved February 21, 2007 from: http://www.justice.gc.ca/en/dept/pub/harassment/harassment.html

Management Issues. (August 20, 2004). *Beware the corporate psycho*. Retrieved July 15, 2007 from http://www.management-issues.com/2006/8/24/research/beware-the-corporate-psycho.asp

Management Issues. (May 5, 2005). *Do employers encourage corporate psychopaths?* Retrieved July 15, 2007 from; http://www.management-issues.com/2006/5/25/blog/do-employers-encourage-corporate-psychopaths.asp

Perrin, K., DeDominic, P. (2007). *Effective Interviewing Techniques*. Retrieved July 14, 2007 from SCORE website: http://www.score.org/hr_3.html

Personnel Today. (February 28, 2006) *HR highlighting bullies in the workplace*. Retrieved January 25, 2007 from: http://www.personneltoday.com/Articles/2006/02/28/34116/hr-highlighting-bullies-in-the-workplace.html

Peters, T.J., Waterman, R.H. (2004). *In search of excellence. Lessons from America's best run companies*. N.Y.: Collins.

Randall, P. (1997). *Adult bullying: Perpetrators and victims*. London & New York: Routledge.

CHAPTER EIGHT

What Employees Can Do

Is it possible to bully proof the work environment? Can employees engage in effective defensive and offensive maneuvers to minimize the effects of workplace warfare? At this time the jury is out on this question. Some authors believe there are things that employees can do to resist being attacked and mistreated in the workplace and others believe that there is very little that can be done without the backing of more senior managers – backing that is in short supply in some organizations.

Some writers suggest that early flight is the best option, while others recommend fighting fire with fire. A range of possible responses will be discussed in this chapter, and it is up to individual employees to determine whether or not any of these solutions might work for them. Pros and cons of many of these options will also be discussed to help readers make informed choices about how they might confront those who engage in noxious behavior in the workplace.

One complicating factor is the often debilitating effects on individuals who are targeted for mistreatment. Depending upon the severity and duration of the harassment that employees have endured, some may be unable to take effective action. Some employees suffer such serious mental and physical health consequences because of their mistreatment that even considering different options may be difficult. For these employees, it is best to seek mental health counseling and medical assistance before considering how to proceed.

For those employees who have begun to be targeted, there are several possible actions that they can consider taking.

Document, Document, Document!

Most of the literature suggests that it is important for employees who are being bullied to keep a journal or some type of written record of the date, time, nature, type, and frequency of whatever psychological harassment is occurring, also detailing what the employee has attempted to do to stop the behavior. This should contain as much detail as possible, including the names of any witnesses, and what the outcome was. Since psychological warfare is defined as a pattern of behavior, it is important to carefully document this pattern, what form it takes, and what, if anything is done about it.

In documenting, it is important to state the facts without editorial comment. Being harassed is very difficult to handle emotionally, but as much as possible, employees should try to keep their emotions out of the documentation, by simply stating exactly what occurred. A private diary can detail the feelings that accompanied the harassment, and/or the distress and negative health effects that may have occurred.

Employees are urged to keep copies of memos, faxes, e-mails, letters, or any other type of written documentation that shows that harassment has occurred. Where it is possible to save voice mails, this should also be done.

If an employee is suffering negative health effects because of the harassment, it would be wise to visit a doctor and/or therapist and discuss these effects, seeking assistance to address them. Asking a third party professional or employee assistance counselor to simply note that you have reported this, and asking for any medical or psychological reports that would substantiate that the employee is suffering ill effects because of the harassment would also be important.

If there is a workplace policy, the employee should follow it to the letter in reporting the harassment, using the documentation to illustrate its nature. Where there is no workplace policy, the harassment should be reported to a direct supervisor, or where the direct supervisor is the harasser, to that person's boss. If the complaint is not appropriately addressed, discounted or minimized the employee should advance to the next level of management (CCOHS, 2001).

The Best Defense is a Good Offense

Some writers suggest that the best way to confront psychological warfare is head on. Others suggest fighting fire with fire. Still others say not to touch it directly but to ask those with the authority to act to address it. Still others say that the best option is to get out of the situation by whatever means necessary.

What this means is that there are a broad range of options, none of which are guaranteed to succeed in every situation. A great deal depends upon the individuals involved, and the situation – organizational climate, culture, peer support and especially whether or not management is prepared to confront the problem.

Every reader will have to assess for her or himself which possible approach makes the most sense.

The Direct Approach

Some writers suggest that the best approach is to be direct. When the person begins the harassment, raise your hand in the "stop" position, and simply say, "stop, I am not prepared to be subjected to this kind of treatment. I want you to stop – fill in the blanks – shouting at me, belittling me in front of my peers, falsely accusing me of things I did not do, personally attacking me, trying to make me look like a fool in front of my co-workers, constantly scrutinizing me, subjecting me to standards not applied to others, tampering with my belongings, failing to give me the information I need to do my job".

If you do not feel comfortable confronting the person alone, take a union rep, supervisor, or fellow worker with you. By publicly telling the person that her or his behavior is unacceptable and you want it to stop, you do establish a boundary that you are telling the person not to cross. Then, if they continue, you have grounds to put your demand in writing, copied to a more senior person.

Individualized Responses to Different Bully Types

In an earlier chapter different types of bullies were described. Each "type" has a different objective in bullying others in the workplace. The competitive bully wants what someone else has, usually their position, status, or popularity. The openly hostile bully likes to control others through fear. The thrill seeking bully likes to stir up trouble for entertainment value, while the self-absorbed or narcissistic and personality-disordered bullies have mental health problems that likely require some intervention, or at least supportive counseling in a therapist's office. Their inability to maintain relationships that are positive and show honest concern for others is extremely limited. Psychopathic bullies do not have the feelings that others possess, and generally have only one goal in mind – getting whatever it is that they want.

Someone who is dealing with a competitive bully who is trying to get their job may wish to label what is happening – tell the bully that you know that is the game he or she is playing, and if they really want to get ahead they might consider fostering more positive work relationships instead of operating on jealousy and envy. Labeling a process like this is akin to exposing the bully to public view, and labeling them as their own worst enemy in the workplace. The bully will likely deny that that is what they are doing, but providing them with clear examples of their undermining behavior and telling them that it is being interpreted by the target and others as being the result of being overly ambitious, may result in some bullies retreating back to their corners.

Openly hostile bullies want control very badly. Taking control away from them will infuriate them, and cause them to attempt other means of regaining control, but employees who wish to obtain some degree of satisfaction in stopping this kind of bully can best do so by confronting the bully publicly, and telling her or him that you will not tolerate being mistreated and shouted at, and that you want the behavior to stop. If it does not stop, you have the option of saying "I will not put up with this kind of treatment" and walk out. Follow up by filing a formal complaint with a senior manager.

A word of caution here. This will only work if a company has reasonable policies prohibiting this kind of bullying, and there are managers in place willing to address the issue. If not, the best option would be for an employee to seek the support of co-workers who must also live with the bully's abusive behavior. Going as a group to senior management will often be more successful in a situation like this, since it tends to break down senior management's denial of the problem.

Thrill seeking bullies need to be kept busy with other stimulating activities. Trying to get this type of bully involved in extra-curricular activities where they can obtain stimulation without doing too much damage is the recommended option. Some can be persuaded to find stimulation in intrigues involving movie stars, going gambling. bar hopping, or attending car races. Some can be "hooked on" Internet games and chat lines. Anything that a target can do to encourage the person to seek stimulation elsewhere will be helpful. One office convinced a thrill seeking bully to run for public office. Other co-workers helped the office bully to "find herself" in community theatre where she could be in a different kind of limelight. The goal is to get the person's needs for stimulation met in a variety of forums to reduce the amount of intrigue and rabble rousing he or she will stir up in the office.

Narcissistic bullies – those whose level of self-absorption knows no bounds, are more difficult to redirect, because their focus is entirely on themselves. Perhaps the most difficult situation for a narcissistic bully to deal with is employees who establish boundaries. "I'd love to talk, but I have work to do". "I'd love to help out, but I'm pretty swamped right now". It is important to establish boundaries with narcissistic bullies to avoid being sucked dry by their constant demands for attention and help. Narcissistic bullies love "rescuers" – people who will help them out while they go their merry ways. Not allowing oneself to be used is the best way to deal with a narcissistic bully. Realizing that you are not going to listen to them talk about themselves, do their work, or flatter their egos, they will quickly move on to someone who will.

Personality disordered bullies have often come from abusive family backgrounds. They are likely to seek and need approval, and will become very volatile when faced with rejection or abandonment by others. In these situations, they can become quite vindictive. The best approach with personality disordered bullies is to simply keep things light – smile, compliment them on something, chat a bit, then move on. Confronting these individuals, or giving them the impression that you are judging them will cause them to retaliate or become explosive. Lacking boundaries and impulse control, things can quickly spiral out of control. While it is not necessary to walk on eggshells around them, keeping things light and matter of fact will often provide some relief.

Psychopathic bullies are more difficult to deal with. Utterly lacking empathy, being glib and superficially charming, targets may be drawn to them in spite of themselves. Once a target knows he or she is dealing with a psychopathic bully, the best approach is usually to remove oneself from the person's sphere of influence. Psychopathic bullies usually leave a wasteland in their wake – ruined relationships, organizations, and individuals who feel destroyed and unsure that they will ever recover. Because of the potential for violence, any target who is being threatened should report the threat to the police. Anyone dealing with a psychopathic bully who feels physically threatened should attempt to extricate themselves from the situation as quickly as possible. Where there is clear evidence of wrongdoing or unethical conduct, an anonymous note to senior management telling them to look into what is occurring may be the best option.

Fighting Fire With Fire

Often harassers use the kinds of tactics that they themselves fear most. Someone with a fragile self-concept will often belittle others publicly to make themselves look tough or strong. By responding publicly and saying their belittling behavior is unacceptable, you have taken some of the wind out of the person's sails.

Keep in mind though, that if you are dealing with a personality disordered bully, or a psychopathic bully, you may be confronting someone who thrives on conflict and will be better at it than you are. Expect that person to come back with even worse abuse. If that happens, you can simply say, "I'm not going to take this", and leave, resorting to Plan B, which is a more formal complaint to someone more senior.

If you have any concerns about the person who is bullying you escalating into physical violence, the best option is to either remove yourself from the line of fire, by requesting a stress leave, asking for a transfer, or seeking another position, or ask a more senior person to confront the problem. If a direct threat has been made against you, consider calling the police.

Do Not Retaliate!

Some targets have decided to fight back using the bully's own tactics. They have returned fire by placing them under scrutiny, starting rumors about them, belittling their efforts, or trashing them on Facebook or other Internet sites. Unfortunately, should the target ever decide to file a formal complaint, the bully will likely use these actions against the target.

However, using some covert means is not off the table. Anonymously leaving an article in the boss's mailbox on how to better manage staff, or an article on psychological harassment on a bullying co-worker's desk, has sometimes worked wonders.

One of the major difficulties facing managers who try to confront psychological harassment in the workplace happens when bullied employees retaliate. This makes it very difficult to establish who is the harasser and who is the harassee.

Furthermore, bullies who thrive on conflict will use retaliation as a reason to further escalate their behavior, justifying their actions by suggesting that it is they who are being targeted. Some employees have ended up facing sanctions themselves when they have retaliated against a harasser, thereby providing their tormenter with more reason to attempt to provoke them, and continue the harassment.

Retaliation, as tempting as it may be, may well be the worst thing that a targeted employee can do.

Consider Getting Legal Advice

In some Canadian jurisdictions courts have found that a hostile and embarrassing work environment may constitute "constructive dismissal" of a targeted employee. This has been particularly true where obscene language and public humiliation have been part of the harassment. This has been true whether or not the abusive treatment came from managers, supervisors or someone's co-worker.

According to Blaikie (Winter, 2005) even in unionized workplaces: "Arbitrators have upheld disciplinary actions against employees who have acted contrary to policies forbidding "harassment" in the workplace. While generally agreeing that "harassment" requires a course of conduct extending over a period of time, arbitrators have also recognized that a single incident of sufficient seriousness, or a series of incidents all occurring on the same day, can warrant discipline. Discipline has been upheld for harassment directed either at fellow bargaining unit employees or at persons outside the bargaining unit, such as contractors".

Adams (October 11, 2006) reports "A civilian member of the RCMP in the corrections sector was awarded $550,000 in a constructive dismissal suit. After complaining his boss was drinking on duty, the employee was bullied, ridiculed and taunted for years until he no longer felt safe at work. Arbiters found he'd been bullied to the point he was no longer employable".

Another case involving the RCMP was recently settled with an award for $950,000.00 in damages. In this case "a former RCMP constable was said to have suffered such severe psychological harm as a result of persistent harassment by the commander of her detachment, that doctors doubt that she will ever be able to work again at any full-time job".

Other cases have involved features of psychological harassment, including excessively staring at another employee, shouting or name calling, unwanted physical contact, holding someone to a higher standard than other employees, and subjecting them to more criticism, or a higher level of supervision.

Doorey (2005) has raised the issue of "fair dealing" in the employment relationship, and says that the implied duty of employers to treat employees with "decency, civility, respect, and dignity" has been implied in Canadian case law.

Survival Strategies: Control What You Can Control

If you have to keep your job, have few other options, and no means of escape, you may still have options that will help you to survive and rise above a toxic work environment. One of these is focusing on what you can control in your work environment, and letting go of what you are unable to control. In Ontario, there is Health and Safety legislation in place. A call to the Ministry of Labour, Health and Safety division may be a way to initiate an investigation of a workplace rife with harassment. Filing this kind of complaint affords employees some protection against future harassment.

Seek Professional Help

If your organization has a benefits plan, consider seeing a psychologist, especially one who specializes in cognitive-behavioral or interpersonal therapy. If you are unable to change the bully, you are still able to control and change your own reactions to the bully

You can learn to block negative thoughts, transform negative self talk into positive affirmations, make slight changes to your own communication style that can produce big changes in how you relate to others, and they to you. If you are able to do this, it may actually make a bully's behavior less satisfying for her or him.

A therapist may be able to help you to better understand and manage what about the bully's actions trigger your feelings of fear and self-doubt, thereby helping to alter your reactions. While we cannot change others, we are always in charge of ourselves and our own reactions and feelings.

Seeing someone for external support, has the added advantage of symbolically forcing your organization to provide some assistance to you, even if it is only through the benefits package that it provides. Furthermore, having a therapist document the damage to your mental health of having to work in an environment poisoned by psychological warfare may benefit you should you later decide to take legal action.

Build a Strong Social Support System

Bullies win when they succeed in isolating their targets from others. Whether or not your organization has a benefits package that pays for a psychologist or other mental health professional to help you to preserve your mental health, you can still seek support from a non-profit mental health agency that offers counseling at low to no cost, or visit a physician who offers psychotherapy covered by state-funded health insurance.

If all of this fails, consider confiding in a trusted friend and asking for her or his help to problem solve the situation, or just listen and offer you some support. Sometimes you have to be specific in asking friends for their help and in asking for the kind of help that you need.

It is important, when being bullied or otherwise targeted, to let family and friends know what is happening, while asking for their support, advice, and understanding. When those close to us know that something is amiss, but feel shut out of the process, they may feel that we are angry or upset with them and actually add to the problem. Telling them you need their help and explaining what is happening to you, can assist in building a social support system that can help to offset the debilitating effects of workplace psychological warfare. The simple act of being affirmed outside the workplace can be a lifesaver for someone who is feeling hopeless, useless, and in large part, defenceless.

Research has shown that social support, defined as: "the beneficial elements resulting from social relationships, including: emotional aid (empathy); instrumental and concrete aid; information (counselling, mentorship); accompaniment; and/or reinforcement of a sense of belonging and solidarity" (Bouchard et al, 2006), is important in the maintenance of mental health, prevention of illness, disability and death, and in increased resilience (Thoits, 1986; Kawachi and Berkman, 2001; House, 1981; Cohen and Wills, 1985).

Furthermore some research is also showing that helping others is good for our own health and well being (Brown, 2003). Having other interests in the form of volunteer work in an accepting and validating environment outside of the workplace can act as a buffer to the attacks on your self-esteem.

It is important to arrange a "circle of support" so that no one person is the only social support system that we have. Because of the extremely destructive effects of psychological warfare in the workplace, it will be necessary to have several friends and family members that a targeted employee can rely on to problem solve with, or to just listen empathically. The healing power of empathy helps enormously to counter the hurtful effects of workplace warfare. When fighting a psychological war, it is important to have "comrades in arms".

Distract Yourself

One of the worst things a targeted employee can do is engage in rumination. Rumination is when certain thoughts preoccupy us again and again in a compulsive way. When we say "I can't stop thinking about this", we are ruminating. Rumination makes bullying worse because it constantly reinforces its negative effects. One of the best things someone who is being targeted can do is stop the rumination process. The best way to do this is through the introduction of competing thoughts and behaviors – things that do not allow you to do them, and ruminate at the same time.

Psychological warfare works best when it takes over our thoughts, feelings, and behavior. Being able to alter any one of these three renders it less effective.

By focusing on things that have always brought enjoyment outside of work – dancing, gardening, painting, attending theatre, sports activities that require focus – those being targeted can refuse to allow negative thoughts, feelings, and behavior to rule their lives, thereby weakening the effects of psychological warfare.

Whatever activity brings enjoyment and prevents rumination can be considered another weapon in the counter-offensive against psychological warfare.

Pamper Yourself

One of the goals of most bullies is to hurt another person and make them feel unworthy. This goal can be thwarted if those being targeted take special care of themselves. There are many ways to do this including the use of alternative therapies and activities that help heal body, mind, and spirit.

By focusing on building enjoyable exercise like walking, running, bike riding, swimming, or playing competitive sports into a weekly routine, some have found their stress levels greatly reduced.

Others have taken up yoga or meditation finding ways to soothe themselves and build calmer, more in-control feelings.

Still others have used creative visualization and self hypnosis to train themselves to be calmer and non-reactive when bullies try to push their buttons.

An old Gestalt therapy trick of talking to a chair as if the bully was sitting in it, telling the person what you really think of them, has been empowering for some.

Others have decided to start taking B complex vitamins to help them to fight stress and build emotional strength, while also focusing on introducing more fruits and vegetables into their diets, and reducing refined sugar and flour. This aids in reducing inflammation in the body and helps to calm the mind.

If your organization's health plan pays for massage and physiotherapy for stressed muscles, consider booking regular sessions and use the time to relax and rejuvenate – at the insurance company's expense.

Some have sought the services of homeopaths and naturopaths to help them to find remedies to fight stress and negative thinking. Others have taken remedies like valerian to help them to sleep.

Whatever method you choose, it will help to fight back and counter the effects of psychological warfare that you are experiencing.

Re-Build Your Self Worth

Everyone has strengths – things that they are especially good at. Now is the time to capitalize on these. Use your strengths to build a small business outside of work, where your skills and knowledge are valued. Do volunteer work that brings a sense of satisfaction and allows you to be with positive people and make new friends and contacts. Help out a friend and bask in the good feelings of having done so.

Take a course that you are interested in, and feel the satisfaction of getting a good grade and making new friends in the process. Go to a conference or workshop and learn something new while having your thoughts and ideas validated by others.

Learn a new skill that you have always wanted to learn – anything from woodworking to home decorating, then put your new talent to work.

Start reading motivational self-help books. Sometimes the ideas found in these can help someone to change their life's course or greatly alter their perception of situations.

Do the things that make you feel good, in the presence of people who you like. Nothing fights the negative effects of psychological warfare, like the positive effects of self-worth. Bullies get frustrated when no matter what they throw at you, it seems to have no effect. Maintaining your positive self image during difficult times, may, in fact, so frustrate a bully, and damage her or his sense of control, that they decide to leave you alone. Mission accomplished.

Use Humour

While it is very difficult to find humour when feeling besieged and depressed, those who can have found it enormously helpful. Besides, most bullies hate to be laughed at. One targeted employee decided to use humour to fight her bullying boss. Whenever he tried to belittle her in front of her peers, she whipped out a red clown nose and put it on, commenting that it must be hard for him to work with a clown like her. Everyone's laughter took the wind out of his sails and he stalked out of the room.

Start with some of the humorous self help books on the market like "How To Work For An Idiot: Survive and Thrive Without Killing Your Boss" by John Hoover. Or Roberta Cava's book on "Dealing With Difficult People: How To Deal With Nasty Customers, Demanding Bosses, and Annoying Co-Workers".

Go ahead, be a bit impish and leave your book somewhere where your boss will see it, if you feel it will send the message and be safe to do so. If you don't, feel free to copy a few pages and leave them in her or his mailbox. People who are cruel or unkind to others need to know that their behavior can be labeled and identified, and that it is not appreciated.

Each of us will have our own personal favorites, but books like these can sometimes help us to regain our perspectives and laugh at our situations, while learning some new communication tricks that may also help us to frustrate the bullies in our lives.

Whichever of these methods you choose, it will help to improve your situation and reduce the effects of psychological warfare. While not fighting fire with fire, it may be fighting fire with water, which, as we all know, may be even more effective.

REFERENCES

Adams, S. (October 11, 2006). Workplace bullying hitting bottom lines. *Business Edge,* 6(23). Retrieved February 21, 2007 from: http://www.businessedge.ca/article.cfm/newsID/13969.cfm

Blaikie, H. (Winter, 2005). *Psychological harassment in the workplace.* Retrieved July 17, 2007 from: http://www.heenanblaikie.com/fr/expertise/publications/item?id=492

Bouchard, L., Roy, J.F., van Kemenade, S. (2006). *Social capital and health: Maximizing the benefits.* Health Canada. Retrieved July 22, 2007 from: http://www.hc-sc.gc.ca/sr-sr/pubs/hpr-rpms/bull/2006-capital-social-capital/2006-capital-social-capital-2_e.html

Brown, S. (2003). An altruistic reanalysis of the social support hypothesis: The health benefits of giving. *New Directions for Philanthropic Fundraising,* 42, 49 – 57.

CCOHS (Canadian Centre for Occupational Health and Safety. (2001). *Violence in the workplace prevention guide.* 2nd Edition.

Canadian Centre for Occupational Health and Safety. (2007). *Bullying in the workplace.* Retrived July 17, 2007 from http://www.ccohs.ca/oshanswers/psychosocial/bullying.html

Cohen, S, Wills, T.A. (1985). Stress, social support, and the buffering hypothesis. *Psychological Bulletin,* 5, 310-357.

Doorey, D.J. (2005). Employer bullying: Implied duties of fair dealing in Canadian employment contracts. *Queen's Law Journal.* Retrieved February 7, 2007 from: http://www.doorey.com/doorey.pdf

House, J.S. (1981). *Work, stress, and social support.* Reading, MA: Addison-Wesley.

Kawachi, I, Berman, L. (2001). Social ties and mental health. *Journal of Urban Health: Bulletin of New York Academy of Medicine,* 78(3), 458-467.

Thoits, P. (1986). Social support as coping assistance. *Journal of Consulting and Clinical Psychology,* 54(4), 416-423.

CHAPTER NINE

Calling a Truce: Workplace Policies, Procedures and Remedies

Tehrani (2001:81) has said that "an organizational culture that condones, or ignores, a bullying management style, or bullying within teams, not only increases the likelihood that bullying will spread, but also increases the potential for more serious physical violence to occur".

Earlier the costs to organizations of workplace warfare was documented - the loss of good workers, repeated absenteeism, short and long term disability leaves, the negative impact on all employees, and replacing employees who have left. There is, of course, also the problem of organizational liability. It is, therefore, incumbent upon any organization to take the necessary steps to eliminate this problem.

Gerry Smith of WarrenSheppell says that it is vital that organizations act to protect employees from this kind of harassment, especially in the current legal climate. Instituting risk identification methods, "recognizing that there are people who demonstrate abusive and aggressive behavior.. educating employees about risk… instituting no-tolerance policies", and providing support and help to those directly affected, are very useful first steps (Adams, October 11, 2006).

Conflict Resolution Does Not Work On Psychological Workplace Warfare

There remains a belief that if only effective conflict resolution strategies are used by employees and managers, that workplace warfare would be non-existent. Nothing is further from the truth. Workplace warfare is fundamentally different from ordinary workplace conflicts. It is often deeply rooted in the needs of perpetrators to display dominance over others, or to obtain for themselves a position or other benefit that is not rightfully theirs. For this reason the usual rules of communication, and conflict resolution strategies cannot apply when dealing with workplace bullies (Namie & Namie,2003). This is also because the person being targeted does not want to be in the relationship at all, and the bully's goal is not to reach a mutually satisfying resolution.

As previously mentioned bullies often have a need to dominate, control, illegitimately achieve a benefit, or entertain themselves at someone else's expense. Bergman, McIntyre and James (2004:83) have identified individuals with aggressive personalities who feel the need to overcome any opposition they face forcefully, "to fight, to revenge an injury, to attack another with intent to injure or kill, and to oppose forcefully or punish another"(Murray, 1938)

O'Leary-Kelly, Griffin & Glew (1996) and other authors have said that aggressive individuals may also "see some form of aggression as the most effective way to deal with frustrating situations and anger; dislike the target of aggressive acts; desire to inflict some type of harm on the target; and lack strong control over their aggressive impulses" (Bergman, McIntrye and James, 2004:83). In some cases bullying is a symptom of a serious mental health problem that is not amenable to a workplace solution.

The involuntary nature of the bully-target relationship negates the usual assumption that any conflict involves two people, both of whom have equal responsibility for its outcome. Targets generally do not ask to be targeted. As in criminal cases, it is the perpetrators who must be held responsible for their anti-social behavior.

Targets of workplace warfare are literally held in a state of captivity, often unable to escape the attacks. Feeling wounded, vulnerable and distrustful, they will also not wish to engage in conflict resolution with the person who has injured them. They simply want the attacks to stop. Often they want as little contact with the bully as possible.

Conflict resolution can only be practiced in an environment where there is trust and a mutual agreement to try to work it out (Cahr & Abigail, 2006), something that is generally not the case with psychological warfare in the workplace for the reasons mentioned above. Mediation or conflict resolution are, therefore, unlikely to be effective remedies for many kinds of workplace bullying.

In the case of Anne and Marie discussed in Chapter one, Anne tried to get her supervisor to sit down with her and Marie to come to a mutually agreeable conclusion. Marie threatened to "seek representation', and at that, Anne's supervisor ran for cover, likely believing that litigation was in the offing. Having successfully bullied Anne and her supervisor, Marie had the satisfaction of never having had to meet Anne in a face to face discussion with a third party present. This allowed her to continue her bullying tactics, confident in the knowledge that nothing would be done.

Possible Steps To Address Workplace Bullying

Randall (1997:111) has suggested several important steps that organizations can take to address the problem of workplace bullying and harassment. Some of these steps have been discussed in more detail in earlier chapters.

Effective Hiring Policies and Practices

Effective hiring processes can go a long way in preventing bullies from entering a workplace. Using thorough background checks prior to interviews being granted; examining "team fit" through real life exercises with individuals with whom the applicant is likely to be working, seeking the input of the team afterwards; and interviewing a person more than once to obtain several opinions concerning their abilities and interpersonal skills are good ways to attempt to preclude workplace warfare at a later date.

When hiring for administrative and teaching positions, and especially when hiring professionals in the health, human services, emergency services, and law enforcement sectors, it is also vital to check for burnout – defined by Figley (2002:19) as characterized by "irritability, aggression, physical and mental exhaustion.... callousness, pessimism, cynicism, problems in work relationships, and falling off of work performance." Burnout often results from "frustration, powerlessness, and an inability to achieve work goals [as well as] hierarchical pressures, constraints, and lack of understanding". Checking into someone's previous work history, including their relationships with others, and asking questions that require an ability to think creatively and demonstrate innovation, are some ways of attempting to screen out individuals who are burned out. Another way is to provide some negative feedback during the interview to gauge the applicant's reaction to criticism.

Careful checking of references cannot be overstated. Spending some time to ask pertinent interpersonal and work related questions, and to confirm with a reference that the individual has achieved what s/he has claimed are vital.

Codes of Conduct and Policies Specific to Psychological Harassment

New policies and procedures respecting psychological warfare in the workplace should be developed with the involvement of employees and managers at all levels. Seeking input may, in itself, reveal some deep seated issues in departments and units throughout the organization. Involvement of external experts and human resources professionals with specific skills in this area may also be necessary.

A policy prohibiting workplace harassment may be included as part of an existing human rights or health and safety policies or developed as a separate document. This document should be readily accessible to employees on a website, or routinely distributed through internal communication mechanisms. Special provisions in any organization's Human Rights policies should include sections on non-status psychological harassment – meaning harassment that occurs outside of the parameters of most human rights legislation

To be effective, any workplace policy should include a *values statement* that prohibits this kind of harassment and states a commitment to providing a workplace that is both physically and psychologically safe.

A *definition of psychological harassment* and mobbing and its prohibition should be included in any workplace policy.

An employee *Code of Conduct* is vital in providing organizationa direction to employees in how to conduct their work relationships This Code of Conduct should provide specific examples of respectfu and disrespectful types of communications.

Mandatory reporting of psychological harassment by employees t supervisors, and the maintenance of accurate records by supervisor should be included in these policies, as should a requirement tha *any criminal act* such as physical or sexual assault, extortion, fraud stalking or threatening be *reported to the police*. Sample policies and procedures that can be used as starting points, are included as an appendix to this book.

As well as new policies and procedures in this area, it will be important to include *protocols for investigation* that outline how information will be gathered, by whom, and what the steps will be in seeking information from the target and alleged harasser.

Graduated sanctions and steps in progressive discipline should be included in any new policies that outline what consequences are likely to be attached to first time offences, offences that occur more than once, and to different levels of offenses.

Retaliation should also be prohibited, with new consequences attached to any attempts at retaliation.

All of these are necessary components of a credible enforcement approach. Namie (2003:5) has identified the principles of credible enforcement as follows:

- Independent investigation and adjudication by an impartial third party;

- Effective progressive discipline;

- Retaliation prohibition.

Coaching In Less Extreme Circumstances

Namie (2003:5) has said that in cases where the bullying is less extreme, a coaching approach may be tried with the perpetrator. This should include clearly articulated goals for behavioral change, along with required outcomes by a target date. This could be outlined in an "employment-contingent change contract".

Where a workplace bully is simply misguided, having misinterpreted the organizational culture and what it will allow, or where an employee with a good work history is going through a rough patch in her or his personal life, or has suffered health problems or other issues, a contract may be an effective means of changing behavior.

Contracts are unlikely to succeed with personality disordered, psychopathic, thrill seeking, or narcissistic bullies whose behavior is more likely to be deep rooted and require professional intervention.

Intervention For The Target

Where an employee has clearly been harmed as a result of workplace bullying, the organization is responsible for helping to repair the harm. Anyone who has been targeted should be offered psychological first aid in a sensitive and respectful way. This means choice. Anyone who has suffered this type of harm should have the choice of going to see a private therapist paid for by the organization, or an employee assistance counselor. Either service should guarantee confidentiality and effective short or long term follow-up, depending upon what the employee decides. It is vital that choice is provided since rebuilding an employee's sense of empowerment after it has been removed is a matter of basic respect.

A Risk Assessment Instrument

In light of increasing concerns about workplace violence, where either the perpetrator escalates, or the target retaliates, it is important for companies and organizations to have risk assessment tools in place. Interventions should be geared to the level of risk identified by this type of tool.

Heacox and Sorenson (2006) identify the following as behavioral examples with respect to risk for violence. Other, more comprehensive tools are also available that senior managers should explore – possibly with an expert in risk assessment and management.

LOW RISK	MODERATE RISK	HIGH RISK
Employee/manager wastes company resources intended for job completion or engages in other types of unethical conduct	Employee/manager swears at co-workers	Employee/manager slashes someone's tires or sets fires

Employee/manager starts untrue rumors	Employee/manager sabotages co-worker's work i.e. by misfiling documents etc	Employee/manager displays scissors or other work related item that could be used as a weapon during an argument
Employee/manager displays hostility toward others	Employee/manager makes obscene gestures behind another's back	Employee/manager engages in physical or sexual assault against another employee or manager

It is important to recognize that workplace warfare may be overt or covert. Just because it is not witnessed does not mean it is not happening.

Training and Education

A team of specialists may need to be developed within the organization to implement these policies and protocols, or external consultation may be sought initially until the organization can develop its own internal expertise and capacity. Specialists with backgrounds in management, human resources, security, labour relations, health, law, and risk management would be ideal to have onboard.

Once policies and procedures are in effect, anti-harassment training should be adopted to introduce the new policies and procedures and outline the reasons for them.

Staff training provides a good opportunity for senior managers to take part in setting out the organizational expectations concerning appropriate interpersonal behavior in the workplace.

Line managers responsible for dealing with this problem should receive additional training in how to recognize and approach the issue in an effective way. Identifying warning signs should be one aspect of this training, along with ways of talking with employees so that they will disclose workplace harassment.

Since times of important organizational change are often high stress points, managers should be trained in "change management" wherein they learn to reinforce in their employees the importance of team work in achieving new goals. Active listening by managers during a change process is also an important way of modeling appropriate organizational behavior, as are "problem prioritization, negotiation, the defusing of hostility, and designing effective interventions" (Randall, 1997:141). Clarity about the type of change likely to take place, what its impact will be, and the reasons why it is necessary can help to reduce workplace competition and conflict.

Policies and procedures should be periodically distributed to staff, with information on what constitutes "warning signs" of possible workplace warfare. Staff should be encouraged to report these signs to supervisors, or their boss's boss where the boss may be the problem.

One way of doing this may be in the form of an informative brochure that includes the organization's values statement, a definition of workplace bullying and mobbing, some examples of respectful and disrespectful conduct, and some facts about the impact of bullying on both individuals and the organization. A brochure should also include information on where and how to report, including a confidentiality statement, and an outline of the investigative protocol that will follow with a timeline.

In order to break the silence that often occurs in situations of psychological harassment, it is important to encourage employees to come forward. Managers must display their commitment to listening to, and effectively addressing concerns that employees are raising for this approach to succeed.

Exit Interviews

Exit interviews with staff who inexplicably leave their current positions, seek transfers, or leave the organization, may yield useful information concerning workplace bullying. These interviews should be done routinely, especially in departments with high levels of transfers, early retirements, sick leaves, and resignations.

Dr. Joni Johnson (2001), a clinical psychologist and CEO of WorkRelationships also suggests that human resources and senior managers "keep track of turnover statistics by department, by manager, and by unit."

Creating a Culture of Respect and Accountability

Tehrani (2001) suggests some additional "total quality assessment" means of addressing workplace bullying, by promoting the building of a culture of respect in organizations:

- Provide in-house conciliation and mediation opportunities early in the process, before bullying actually occurs;

- 360 degree feedback in performance appraisals, where the opinions of teammates, administrators and where appropriate, customers, are actively sought, as well as the individual's own feedback, and that of their supervisor;

- Team self-assessments which could be done in a focus group or through written assessments that are read by managers. Self-assessments are intended to identify both areas of strength and those needing improvement.

All of the above are intended to assist companies and organizations in implementing effective policies to reduce or eliminate workplace warfare and to disarm the workplace warriors in their midst.

This growing problem, which is causing immeasurable harm to employees and organizations, and more indirectly to families and communities, must be addressed if, as a society, we are to avoid the long term harm and tragic consequences that often accompany it.

Work cannot be isolated from home or community life. What happens in the workplace or the schoolyard can spill over into the broader community, causing increased incivility, hostility, and violence. We all have a role to play in trying to eliminate this type of aggression from our daily lives. This book has been one attempt to do so.

REFERENCES

Adams, S. (October 11, 2006). Workplace bullying hitting bottom lines. *Business Edge,* 6(23). Retrieved February 20, 2007 from: http://www.businessedge.ca/article.cfm/newsID/13969.cfm

Bergman, S.M., McIntyre, M.D., James, L. (2004). Identifying the aggressive personality. *J. of Emotional Abuse: Intervention, Research, and Theories of Psychological Maltreatment, Trauma, and Nonphysical Aggressio,* 4(3/4), 81-93.

Cahn, D.D. & Abigail, R.A. (2006). *Managing conflict through communication.* Boston, MA.: Pearson Allyn and Bacon.

Figley, C. (2002). *Treating compassion fatigue.* U.S.:Brunner Routledge.

Heacox, N.J., & Sorenson, R.C. (Summer, 2006). Aggression in Organizations: Violence, Abuse, and Harassment at Work and in Schools. *Personnel Psychology,* 59 (2), 471–474.

Johnson, J.J. (September 10, 2001). In Bredemeier, K., *On the job.* Retrieved: August 19, 2007 from: http://www.workrelationships.com/site/articles/onthejob.htm

Murray, H.A. (1938). *Explorations in personality.* N.Y.: Oxford University Press.

Namie, G., Namie, R. (2003). *The bully at work.* Naperville, Illinois: Sourcebooks Inc.

Namie, G. (2003). Workplace bullying: Escalated incivility. *Ivey Business Journal Online.* Retrieved August 19, 2007 from: http://www.bullybusters.org/press/ivey.pdf

O'Leary-Kelly, A.M., Griffin, R.W., & Glew, D.J. (1996). Oganization-motivated aggression: A research framework. *Academy of Management Review,* 21(1), 225-253.

Randall, P. (1997). *Adult bullying: Perpetrators and victims.* London & New York: Routledge.

Tehrani, N. (2001). *Building a culture of respect: Managing bullying a work.* London & New York: Taylor and Frances.

APPENDIX A

SAMPLE POLICY

FORBIDDING PSYCHOLOGICAL HARASSMENT

IN THE WORKPLACE

1. Scope and Purpose of the Policy

This policy is intended to protect all employees of ……………………………….. from psychological harassment and mobbing, and to ensure a work environment that is both physically and psychologically safe.

Every employee of ……………………………………. is required to promote and maintain an environment that is free of psychological harassment and mobbing.

Administrative and managerial employees, or others in positions of authority, have the additional responsibility of recognizing and preventing psychological harassment.

2. Objectives of the Policy

This policy is intended to address any form of harassment, abuse of power, or violence in the workplace, in order to promote employees' psychological and physical health, protect their dignity, and encourage harmonious and professional working relationships.

This policy also outlines administrative measures to address the issue of psychological harassment in the workplace, including reporting and investigative protocols, and graduated sanctions to deter it.

3. Definitions

Psychological harassment is defined as any repetitive vexatious behaviour in the form of hostile, inappropriate, and unwanted behavior, comments, actions or gestures that are hostile or unwanted, and negatively affect an employee's dignity, psychological or physical integrity and lead to a harmful work environment for the employee. This encompasses any abuse of authority, including intimidation, threats, blackmail, reprisals, or coercion that occurs when a person improperly uses the power or authority inherent in the person's position to endanger an employee's job, undermine the employee's job performance, threaten the economic livelihood of the employee, or interfere in any other way with the career or physical and psychological health of the employee[1]

One serious incidence of such behaviour may also constitute psychological harassment where it can be shown that this behaviour resulted in a lasting harmful effect on the employee, negatively affecting her or his dignity, or psychological or physical integrity.

Mobbing occurs where a group of individuals repeatedly engages in hostile and unethical behavior that is directed in a systematic manner toward one individual or group of individuals, whose dignity or psychological and physical integrity are negatively affected as a result[2].

Abuse of power or authority means the use of power or authority conferred by a position in a manner that is inappropriate, unprofessional, unethical, or illegitimate, compromising the ability of an employee to complete tasks and meet her or his professional responsibilities, and which may interfere with the continuance of her or his employment without just cause.

The following illustrates, but is not an exhaustive list, of the kinds of conduct that are prohibited by this policy:

- Contemptuous, condescending, ridiculing, or disrespectful conduct, comments, or insinuations in private or public;

- Threats or attempts to intimidate;

- Refusal to share information or withholding of resources required to complete professional responsibilities, or providing erroneous or misleading information;

---

1   This definition is an adaptation of the definition included in Bill C 451: An Act To Prevent Psychological Harassment in the Workplace And Amend The Canada Labour Code, First Reading, September 24, 2003, and the definition included in Quebec legislation respecting psychological harassment in the workplace.

2   This definition is based upon information and research carried out in Sweden by Leymann (1990).

- Insults, gestures, inappropriate jokes, and verbal assaults, including yelling, lashing out, blackmailing or pressure tactics;

- An unusual level of scrutiny or monitoring unrelated to an individual's professional performance;

- Stalking;

- Isolating, ignoring, shunning or silencing without cause;

- Assigning work below an employee's abilities, or removing responsibilities without cause;

- Spreading untrue rumors or gossip;

- Engaging in personal attacks;

- Making false, misleading, or unsubstantiated accusations;

- Public or private attempts to humiliate or embarrass.

4. Prohibition of Retaliation

Anyone who is the subject of a complaint under this policy may not retaliate against a person who uses the policy in a legitimate manner to raise and seek remedy for instances of psychological harassment, mobbing, or abuse of power. Doing so is subject to sanction.

5. Frivolous Complaints

Individuals are prohibited from making complaints without just cause, that are frivolous, lack substance, or are intended to intimidate or cause harm to another person. Doing so is subject to sanction.

6. How To Make An Informal Complaint

Informal complaints may be made to a supervisor, or where the supervisor is the respondent, to that person's supervisor within 90 days. Informal complaints may be made verbally or in writing.

The manager to whom the complaint has been made shall meet with the complainant and respondent, separately or together, taking into consideration the complainant's wishes, within 5 working days of the complaint being made.

The manager will inform both parties of the outcome of the complaint in writing. Should the complaint be found to be justified, the manager will meet with the respondent, setting out clear expectations concerning the respondent's future conduct, or take whatever other measures s/he deems appropriate in the circumstances.

The manager will also arrange assistance for the complainant, depending upon the complainant's wishes and the severity of the harassment or abuse of power.

Nothing in this section precludes the complainant from going forward with a more formal complaint.

7. How to Make A Formal Complaint

Individuals seeking to make a complaint under this policy shall report their concerns in writing within 90 days of the alleged last act of harassment, abuse of power, or violence to...................................... (designate individual or individuals by position)

.... will conduct an investigation that consists of the following:

- Taking statements of fact from both the complainant and respondent;

- Taking the statements of any other individual or individuals who may have witnessed any alleged incidents or actions;

- Question the complainant, respondent and any witnesses;

- Require that all parties to the complaint maintain a strict level of confidentiality;

- Review all written documentation provided by either the complainant or respondent;

- Make a determination within 30 days based upon the preponderance of evidence related to all of the above;

- Inform the complainant and respondent of the decision with reasons.

- Consult with the complainant regarding potential corrective measures.

7. Sanctions

Depending upon the strength of the evidence presented in #6, and the seriousness of the proven allegations, the following sanctions may be applied:

a) Separation of the parties by modifying work or schedules;

b) A verbal reprimand or warning, noted in the employee's file;

c) A written reprimand or warning, noted in the employee's file.

d) A suspension with pay for a length of time determined by the employee's supervisor;

e) A suspension without pay for a length of time determined by the employee's supervisor;

f) Removal from her or his position to another position within the organization;

g) Dismissal;

h) A report to a professional College;

i) Police involvement.

8. Assistance To The Complainant

Where appropriate, assistance in the form of counseling, financial compensation, a change of position, or other actions may be offered to the complainant.

9. Right of Appeal

A respondent may file an appeal of the decision.

The first stage of appeal will be to .... (designate individual by position)

The second and final stage of appeal will be to a tribunal constituted for purposes of hearing the appeal. The tribunal shall consist of.. (designate individuals – no more than 3 – by position).

The tribunal shall hear from both parties and any proposed witnesses. Either party to the complaint shall be allowed to retain representation for purposes of the appeal.

10. Training

Professional training will be provided to both line managers and supervisors handling information complaints, and to individuals designated to receive and investigate formal complaints.

APPENDIX B

SAMPLE EMPLOYEE CODE OF CONDUCT

Employees of .... are expected to conform to the highest ethical standards, treat co-workers, administrators, staff, and customers in a courteous and considerate manner, meet or exceed the requirements of their professions, obey the laws of ...., and refrain from engaging in conduct that would otherwise be considered disreputable or damage the reputation of the organization.

Specifically employees are asked to:

1. Behave in a civil manner to co-workers, supervisors and customers, refraining from causing others discomfort, psychological or physical harm, embarrassment, or loss of dignity.

2. Be aware of their impact on others, and this includes avoiding intimidation, threatening, or coercive conduct.

3. Fulfill their professional responsibilities to the organization, and this includes avoiding insubordination, fulfilling their duties according to their job descriptions, providing good customer service, and refraining from engaging in any unauthorized employment while being paid by the organization to perform their duties, or while on paid benefits related to illness, or while on a leave of absence.

4. Complete their duties in a responsible manner taking into account the reputation of the organization, and addressing any due diligence concerns.

5. Avoid excessive absenteeism.

6. Behave in an honest manner, refraining from theft, fraud, embezzlement and other acts of dishonesty.

7. Provide honest and accurate records and accounts, refraining from falsifying records or documents, or accepting gifts of any kind that would place them in a conflict of interest.

8. Promote a harmonious work environment avoiding behavior that is likely to cause disruption or interfere with others' abilities to perform their duties.

9. Appropriately use computers or other technical equipment as well as codes or passwords.

10. Avoid soliciting other employees for specific causes or fundraising events, or for religious reasons.

11. Maintain professional relationships and boundaries with clients and customers, refraining from engaging in romantic or sexual relationships.

12. Report illegal, unethical, or disruptive behavior to the appropriate supervisor, senior manager, or human resources.